T0192924

ESSENTIAL ESSAYS SERIES 71

Guernica Editions Inc. acknowledges the support
of the Canada Council for the Arts and the Ontario Arts Council.
The Ontario Arts Council is an agency of the Government of Ontario.
We acknowledge the financial support of the Government of Canada.

Hillar Liitoja

THE

CHALLENGE

GUERNICA
EDITIONS
TORONTO • BUFFALO • LANCASTER (U.K.)
2019

Michael Mirolla, editor
Guernica Editions Inc.
Cover design: Magdalena Vasko
Interior design: Rafael Chimicatti
1569 Heritage Way, Oakville, (ON), Canada L6M 2Z7
2250 Military Road, Tonawanda, N.Y. 14150-6000 U.S.A.

Distributors:
University of Toronto Press Distribution,
5201 Dufferin Street, Toronto (ON), Canada M3H 5T8
Gazelle Book Services, White Cross Mills
High Town, Lancaster LA1 4XS U.K.

First edition.
Printed in Canada.

Legal Deposit – First Quarter
Library of Congress Catalogue Card Number: 2019932754
Library and Archives Canada Cataloguing in Publication

Title: The Oulipo challenge / Hillar Liitoja.
Names: Liitoja, Hillar, author.
Series: Essential essays series ; 71.
Description: Series statement: Essential essays series ; 71
Identifiers: Canadiana (print) 20190062266 | Canadiana (ebook)
20190062304 | ISBN 9781771833738 (softcover)
| ISBN 9781771833745 (EPUB)
| ISBN 9781771833752 (Kindle)
Subjects: LCSH: Oulipo (Association)
| LCSH: French literature—Societies, etc.
| LCSH: Literature, Experimental.
Classification: LCC PQ22.O8 L55 2019 | DDC 840.9—dc23

Table of Contents

THE CHALLENGE

What is the Oulipo?

Oulipo … is a secret laboratory of literary structures.
— Noël Arnaud, member since 1961

Oulipo was – is – a seedbed, a grimace, a carnival.
— Susan Sontag

*The Oulipo is not a school; it's a nursery where we force cylinders
into square holes and cubes into round ones while our parents
and proctors aren't looking. Does it work? Depends on the day.*
— François Caradec, member since 1983

*"Only by working within limitations does the master manifest his
mastery," and the limitation, the very condition of any art, is style.*
— Oscar Wilde, in *The Decay of Lying,*
  begins stating his belief by quoting Goethe

* * *

The Oulipo, acronym for *OUvroir de LIttérature POtentielle*
(Workshop for Potential Literature), is a small literary
group dedicated to creating new possibilities for writing. When
put into practice, their innovations have resulted in a fascinating,
highly idiosyncratic body of literature. The starting point for each
endeavour is the use or invention of a set of formal rules, called
restrictions or constraints, which are then scrupulously adhered
to in order to arrive at texts previously inconceivable or
unimaginable. These trammels are invariably of great clarity,

highly inventive and, often, fiendishly challenging – essential in forcing one's mind to the furthest reaches of its intelligence and creativity. The *corpus* of work is exceptionally wide-ranging, from tiny fragments, lists, sentence-series to poems, stories and full-out novels. All compositions belong to (at least) one in a lexicon of hundreds restriction-categories, each bearing its own charming, if not exactly illuminating, appellation: lipogram; perverse; heterosexual rhyme; N + 7; prisoner's restriction; pre-cooked language; asphyxiation; tautogram; corpuscular poem and Canada Dry.

Daniel Levin Becker, member since 2009 – whose thoroughly marvellous *Many Subtle Channels: in praise of Potential Literature* (2012) is a fascinating combination of history and deeply personal memoir while simultaneously a not-always-reverently-questioning reflection on all things Oulipo – says it is – *a sort of literary supper club … a hallowed echo chamber for investigations of poetic form and narrative constraint and the mathematics of wordplay … it has served as the laboratory in which some of modernity's most inventive, challenging, and flat-out baffling textual experiments have been taken … its works, all of them governed in some way by strict technical constraints or elaborate architectural designs, are attempts to prove the hypothesis that the most arbitrary structural mandates can be the most creatively liberating.*

Admitting the difficulties of being overly precise about the Oulipo's nature, Levin Becker is more firm on what it is *not – not a movement, or an -ism, or a school. It does not have an agenda, aesthetic or political or otherwise … it does not purport to tell anyone what literature should or must be. What it does is tell … what literature* could *and* might *be, sometimes by speculation, other times by demonstration.*

Founders

The Oulipo was conceived in September 1960 when Raymond Queneau approached François Le Lionnais for encouragement and advice on the composition of his *A Hundred Thousand Billion Poems*, also titled *100,000,000,000,000 Poems*. These discussions eventually led to a meeting of seven men – writers, scientists, mathematicians – who became the Oulipo's core group to which members were gradually added. The original interest in an overarching understanding of experimental literature, past and present, developed into a new concern – how to amalgamate mathematical concepts with literary creations – which widened into the formulation and application of other rigorous means of shaping the outcome of literary productions.

Queneau (1903-76) had degrees in Greek, Latin and philosophy before he joined the Surrealists, severing his connection, though, five years later after a violent dispute with André Breton. (Interesting to note how Oulipian adherence to severe restrictions is anathema to the Surrealists' foundation-stone of "total liberty.") Soon after, he began collaborating with Georges Bataille as well as starting as lowly manuscript-reader at *Éditions Gallimard*, the grand publishing house. A decade later he had become a respected poet, novelist and essayist as well as a director in *Gallimard*'s classics series. Popular acclaim arrived with the publication of *Zazie dans le Métro* (*Zazie in the Metro*, 1959) with its high-spirited, mouth-should-be-soaped girl spewing glued-together insolences reflecting how word-groups are actually *heard*, not written.

Mathematics had always been an integral part of Queneau's life (as well as the Oulipo's) which, along with his love of Bach's music, led him to further burrow into the workings of formal systems. One early product of these investigations was *Exercices de Style* (*Exercises in Style*, 1947) which pursues the often elliptical telling of a rather banal story in 99 different ways: exhaustive, inventive, ingenious and often amusing if not downright funny. It feels like a super-elongated musical theme and variations.

His 1960 *opus monumental, 100,000,000,000,000 Poems*, can actually be printed comfortably on ten pages, each containing a classic 14-line sonnet. The spectacular number derives from your own relentless constructions as any first line can be followed by any second, then any third, and so on, all versions never deviating from the rhyme-scheme nor grammar's fidelity. By Queneau's calculations, devoting 24 hours per day to its reading would require 190,258,751 years before finally reaching the final iambic pentameter. On the other hand, were you to ride from the beginning to the terminus of Paris Métro's line 5, you would, in far shorter time, arrive at the penultimate station named posthumously in his honour.

* * *

Le Lionnais (1901-84) maintained his youthful involvement with circles magnetized by artists Max Jacob and Jean Dubuffet as he devoted himself to science and mathematics. He ended up trained as a chemical engineer. During World War II he was arrested and tortured as a Resistance-member; while imprisoned he wrote a paper on chess, a life-long ardour reflected in his later collection of over two thousand volumes on the subject. His way of preserving sanity-semblance during some two years in concentration camps was to mentally envision, to the tiniest details, his favourite paintings, an experience he would soon recount in a memoir whose title bears a camp's name, *La Peinture à Dora* (*Painting at Dora*, 1946).

Post-Liberation Le Lionnais worked as a scientist in various posts: at UNESCO, then for the French National Museums and national public-broadcast service before editing a math-reference tome for the national universities. His interest in contemporary mathematics resulted in a published collection of articles, one contributor being none other than Queneau.

Le Lionnais' force lay in theory, contributing little Oulipian writing save for three manifestos – two complete, one not. Levin Becker becomes a little overwhelmed when touching on Le Lionnais – *[his] life is a topic of reverent mystery within the Oulipo. ... A few copies of a manuscript ... which gathers together memoirs and a handful of interviews ... have circulated in the official and unofficial archives, but, even with the savant commentary it has elicited, the man and his thoroughgoing polymathy seem mythically impossible to fully comprehend ...*

Nicolas Bourbaki

In thrall to secrecy, enamoured by enigma's thrill, the non-existent Monsieur Bourbaki's name was chosen as pseudonym by a small group of distinguished young 1930s French mathematicians who set out to reformulate and secure their field's core foundations. The group's formation was in response to a confidence-eroding crisis as the most gifted minds imagined very different philosophical approaches to mathematics' essence: formalism, intuitionism, logicism and platonism. Debates' intensity transcended disagreements over proofs' validity, permissible "uses" of infinity, and degenerated into manifestations of personal hatred. Believing malaise's root lay in the application of insufficient rigour along with complexities' disregard, these purists blamed older mathematicians' calcified mind-sets for clutching out-dated methodologies. In keeping with these beliefs the collaborators insisted on each member's retirement upon reaching fifty, to be replaced by fresher blood.

During their three- or four-times-a-year clandestine meetings of week-or-two-long focused concentration-bursts, they agreed every word of their texts needed all participants' approval. Under these conditions it is surprising the collaborators managed to agree upon even a pamphlet's contents, never mind achieving the feat of nine volumes published 1935-1983. Their work is still considered of some value – though it did lead to America's 1960s "new math" reforms which caused endless bewilderment and consternation amongst schoolchildren and parents alike.

I have never clearly understood the connection between Bourbaki and the Oulipo. Does the relation lie in their avant-garde nature as both sought new approaches to their disciplines? Do audacity, extreme formalism, implacable rigour all contribute to their kinship? Is there significance in Bourbaki's decision to begin rewriting mathematics with the Set Theory, a logic-branch involving collections of objects? By extension, does the imposition of each restrictions-bundle – write a Petrarchan sonnet with no line's first word beginning with a vowel – create a new "set"? We know Queneau and Le Lionnais had Bourbaki – *a counter-model to the Surrealist group* – in mind when founding the Oulipo. Jacques Roubaud (member since 1966), in his introduction to the indispensable, magisterial, often sly and cheeky *Oulipo Compendium* (1998, updated 2005, edited by Harry Mathews and Alastair Brotchie), tells us – *the Oulipo is an homage to Bourbaki and an imitation of Bourbaki.* He then goes on to inform us – *At the same time, it is no less obviously a parody of Bourbaki, even a profanation of Bourbaki.* In Roubaud's view – *Bourbaki's initial plan … is at once serious, admirable, imperialistic, sectarian, megalomaniac, and pretentious.* Clarity eludes me. Perhaps that meets the author's intent. In any case, Oulipians can be writers, mathematicians, writer-mathematicians or mathematician-writers.

Collège de 'Pataphysique

Alfred Jarry, best known for his play *Ubu Roi* (1896) – whose protagonist's tyrannical (and scatological) outrages over only two performances caused a furor similar to *Le Sacre du Printemps* in Paris almost two decades later – was a Symbolist writer whose work became a precursor to wherever you wish to cast your stone: Dada, Absurdism, Surrealism, Futurism, even Postmodernism. As though such influence was insufficient for an artist's lifetime, Jarry also conceived the idea and philosophical concepts of 'Pataphysics, a contraction of a Greek phrase to mean – *that which is above metaphysics.*

In 1948, just over forty years after Jarry's death, the College of 'Pataphysics was founded in Paris by those interested in examining ideas flowing from Jarry's work. Brotchie informs us it is – *a society committed to learned and inutilous research.* "Inutilous" is another way of saying "useless" and the College motto, translated from Latin, is – *I arise the same though changed.*

The essence, meaning and philosophy of 'Pataphysics is so abstract and elusive there apparently exist multiple dozens of definitions. Jarry himself called it, variously – *a science of exceptions and imaginary solutions; a science of equivalence and imperturbability* – dealing with – *the laws which govern exceptions and will explain the universe supplementary to this one.* American Heritage Dictionary takes its stab – *'pataphysics is a branch of philosophy or science that examines imaginary phenomena that exist in a world beyond metaphysics.* I find Brotchie's view particularly endearing – *'Pataphysics passes easily from one state of apparent definition to another. Thus it can present itself under the aspect of a gas, a liquid or a solid.* The final word, however, goes to Levin Becker – *anyone who claims he or she understands the* Collège de 'Pataphysique *is probably lying.*

Roger Shattuck, in an introduction to Jarry's posthumously-published *Exploits and Opinions of Dr. Faustroll, Pataphysician* – dealing with an anti-philosopher, born at age 63, who hallucinates while gliding through Paris in a sieve – suggests the eel-slippery 'pataphysics core principle is – *the virtual or imaginary nature of things as glimpsed by the heightened vision of poetry or science or love can be seized and lived as real.* In other words, with proper mind- and senses-awareness you need not take LSD to have that earth-shattering life-altering epiphany – although perhaps it was merely the impoverished Jarry's passionate wish that the other-worldly effects of drugs and his beloved absinthe could be achieved without spending a single *sou.*

Jarry insisted on the pre-P apostrophe in order to avoid its consideration as a paronym, a word which sounds like a different word (homonym) or words-group. Apostrophe's presence, however, seems pointless as it has no effect on the word's pronunciation and does nothing to prevent mis-hearings such as *patte à physique* (physic's paw), *pas ta physique* (not your physics) and *pâte à physique* (physics pastry dough). 'Pataphysics-practitioners (pataphysicians, pataphysicists) are apparently immune to such aural disfiguration and thus require no apostrophe.

College-members all have their appropriate position in the hierarchy, seemingly determined by association's duration, from the novice Dataire to its most senior, the Vice-Curator, Her

Magnificence Lutembi who, in real life, is a crocodile. Queneau was a Transcendent Satrap whereas Le Lionnais was (it seems merely) a regent. The *Compendium* shows the former pinning the *Ordre de la Grande Gidouille* on the latter, the *gidouille* being College's emblem representing the energy-force residing in Ubu's intestines which flows through his navel and enfolds the whole universe before returning home.

The College went into abeyance from 1975-2000, a time known as "the occultation," before resuming its activities and publications during their self-devised thirteen-month calendar, my personal favourites being Ha Ha, Debraining and Bicycle pedal. An organization of such piquant bizarreness certainly attracted its share of fascinating artists and you will undoubtedly be familiar with certain illustrious members: Arrabal, Buñuel, Duchamp, Max Ernst, Escher, Ionesco, Umberto Eco, Miró, Picabia, Man Ray … and three brothers Marx.

The Oulipo revealed itself in December 1961 with a publication in the College's roughly-quarterly periodical. Dossier 17 outlines, in compact form, the group's interests and aims along with some examples of potential techniques and procedures. The workshop became a subset of the College's subcommission on Epiphanies and Ithyphanies, itself a subcommission of the Commission of the Unpredictable; weeks later it moved on to being a subcommittee of *Acrote*; not much later it became a subcommittee unto itself. Ithyphanies derives from a god-statue with a hard-on, *Acrote* ostensibly refers to humanity's grandest goal – and by now I imagine you need know nothing more about *Collège de 'Pataphysique*'s endless convolutions, save, perhaps, they performed some farsighted services such as publishing Ionesco's *Bald Soprano*, now acknowledged the quintessential absurdist play, which until that point was the recipient of countless rejection-slips.

Membership

Oulipians: rats who construct the labyrinth from which they plan to escape.
    — Raymond Queneau

The members of the Oulipo are characters in an unwritten novel by Raymond Queneau.
    — Jacques Roubaud

* * *

Despite countless hours perusing the *Compendium* – fascinating, engrossing, addictive, after the brief introduction to be read not as a book but dipped into like an encyclopaedia – I have yet to uncover how one becomes a member. Is there a long-awaited midnight-hour triple-knock on one's door? Does a courier place an envelope in one's hand and upon opening one finds the invitation – but written in "Oulipese"? If you can decode the message do you become a member? Or must you accept in language mimicking invitation's restrictions? Do you send a splendid sample of your work containing newly-invented restrictions along with an admission-requesting note? Perhaps all you do is call the Oulipo Head Office – which I don't think actually exists. (This reminds me of the young Susan Sontag wishing to write for *Partisan Review*, bumping into one of its editors at a cocktail party who told her – *All you have to do is ask.* She no doubt didn't miss a beat – *Well, I'm asking.*)

Whether the process is simple or fraught, straight-forward or necromantic, one must consider carefully before joining this rarefied group: membership is onerous. Once a member, always a member. You cannot be expelled. Nor can you resign. Death will terminate your life but not your membership. Upon reflection it was decided this rule risked being considered "unduly coercive" so a solution was found. You might call it a "final" solution: suicide. Not any old euthanasia-enactment, however, but one with specific purpose and procedure – *suicide may be committed in the presence of an officer of the court, who then ascertains that, according to the Oulipian's explicit last wishes, his suicide was intended to release him from the Oulipo and restore his freedom of manoeuvre for the rest of eternity.*

Moments after writing the above two paragraphs I became consumed with curiosity and logged, for the first time, onto the Oulipo website. There was no "contact us" link but, to my flawed French, there seemed – within the grand Parisian *Bibliothèque nationale de France* – to be a sumptuous room devoted to all things Oulipo called, no doubt owing to a patron's largesse, the *Olivier* Salon. I clicked on the address and requested the librarian in charge to tell me – or find out from an actual member – how one joins this band of restrictive wordsmiths. I quickly received a reply and you might imagine my delight finding out this Olivier Salon was not some well-appointed library-cranny but the name of an actual member of the Oulipo! A lively back-and-forth ensued with the welcoming and inquisitive Olivier who kindly answered all my questions in workmanlike English, a language the French seem to regard with a mixture of distaste and horror.

It turns out the one way to guarantee *not* becoming a member is to request becoming one – and over the years this categorical rejection, even to probably suitable candidates, has thumped again and again. A writer may submit work for consideration. Members may themselves land upon writings sufficiently interesting to be passed around and discussed. If material is found stimulating, the writer is invited to meet with members and a conversation about her ideas, particular restraints and work ensues. Olivier explains – *Then, we let the time go, many months … as [the] Oulipo members are for life, we have to choose [someone] who is interesting for literature with constraints and a nice person too.* After the appropriate time for reflection has passed a vote is taken – and all (living) members must unanimously be in favour of "co-opting" this new soul into the eternal circle. Then it is simply a matter of formal notification and waiting for a positive response before declaring a person the newest member.

In the early years, however, the Oulipo was run somewhat differently. Levin Becker tells us Queneau – *had basically autocratic control over [selecting] the first generation of recruits.* The later-adopted unanimity-principle had the drawback of opening doors to petty meanness as one-vote denials *do* occur. Writer and historian François Caradec, first invited as guest to an "audition-lunch" back in 1964, was denied admission solely on account of prickly cactus-devotee Latis – not to worry if his name doesn't ding as he used more pseudonyms than you have fingers and possibly toes – who, well, just bore him some grudge. Poor Caradec had to wait for Latis' interment – and then another decade – before finally being embraced by all members in 1983.

Surely it is an event of singular distinction and honour to be invited to join the Oulipo – Levin Becker likens it to instantly becoming a family-member – however there are those who refused the co-optation and at least one who studiously eluded invitations to that "audition-lunch." Living Oulipians may be divided into two groups, those active and those not, the former graded to the latter owing to old age, non-France residency or just having soured on the whole venture. Speaking of family, right from the beginning it was felt all those active should easily fit around a large dinner-table, all seated comfortably in visual and aural range of each other.

At the moment I count 41 members – five women, eight non-French – with 21 deceased. The names you are most likely to recognize both fall in the latter category: Italo Calvino and Marcel Duchamp.

Meetings

S tarting a few years post-inception, the Oulipo has held monthly meetings, a schedule strictly adhered to: every month, every year, no exceptions. They normally take place in members' domiciles; the following meeting's date is determined often at each one's end; no quorum necessary but there is an agenda, punctiliously observed by the President who "runs" the event; minutes are taken with varying degrees of precision and then preserved. So these get-togethers are, despite strict agenda-adherence, pretty informal, even intimate, with *soupçons* of mischief and crankiness. Levin Becker feels the minutes – *don't capture the Thanksgiving-dinner overtones of affection and bickering* – and being particularly well-versed in them, due to extensive archival work, is to be trusted when he feels – *serious business and serious prattle appear to have remained in roughly constant equilibrium throughout the workshop's evolution.*

The President, over aperitifs, will cobble together the agenda, always beginning with "*création*" – otherwise there's no point to meeting – to be followed by "*rumination*" and "*érudition*" before winding down with those mundane practical considerations which bedevil any outfit.

The crucial *création* component deals with any Oulipian's recent writing, fresh ideas for constraints, variations on previous ones; *rumination* has amusement's possibility as Ian Monk (member since 1998) speaks of it as – *a safe section for new members who often eagerly announce some brilliant idea they think they have just had only to be told that Georges Perec had already thought of it years ago.* Lesser emphasis is placed today on *érudition* which concerns felicitously-coined "anticipatory plagiarism", a reference to numerous writers – such as Arnaut Daniel, Lewis Carroll, Raymond Roussel and Edgar Allan Poe – who used Oulipian techniques well before the Oulipo was ever conceived. *Érudition* received particular attention in the early years as members wished to lay an intellectual underpinning, what Levin Becker calls – *articulating a lineage in which the group's explorations could be inscribed* – going on to explain these writers' – *elaborations on technique and form gave modern experimental literature its sense of self.* We are all aware that sonnets, for example, have been written for centuries in confines of differing forms; however, early Oulipians sniffed out work by authors not remotely illustrious as the above-mentioned, my favourite being the fellow who, annoyed by 1804 French civil code's tedious prose, apparently rewrote the entire thing in rhyming verse …

Meetings also provide the ideal environment where guests may share their work, ideas and preoccupations while getting a sense of the actual people they might one day be confreres with. And, of course, it is the very same sanctuary in which Oulipians listen, question and vet the potential newcomer.

We can be certain drinking did not end with those aperitifs served during agenda-setting and seeing most Oulipians are French it should come as no surprise wining and dining have always been an integral part of each meeting. Poet and mathematician Jacques Roubaud remembers – *lots of [the original] Oulipians were great drinkers.* From the present crop, top prize seems to go to Monk, described by Frédéric Forte (member since 2005) as – *le punk de l'Oulipo* – who in agreeable company apparently drinks, as the French so charmingly put it, "like a hole."

Though a native New Yorker, Harry Mathews (member since 1972) spent enough time in France to take pride in the nation's venerable cuisine – and not only via osmosis as his evident culinary assiduity generated a true gourmet. He seems to have been hardly alone as Levin Becker wonders which Oulipian could best – *have schooled whom on the art of fine dining.*

One of the most extraordinary meetings occurred in April 1990, *chez* Mathews, the only Oulipian present, with the sole guest being a math research fellow at Princeton's renowned Institute for Advanced Study (IAS). For years I have been entranced by proceedings' extravagance. Once *création* and *érudition* had been dispensed with, the fellow invited all Oulipians to visit IAS for a conference with its literary and math members, topic to be chosen by the guests: round-trip by (now-extinct) supersonic Concorde; lodgings at luxurious Carlyle; daily $500 per diems and limousine service all provided. Due to lack of quorum – I thought meetings had no quorum – Mathews was obliged to most courteously decline.

The matter, however, was not over. Mathews made a counter-offer: all IAS members invited to meet with the Oulipians, topic again to be chosen by guests; round-trip again by Concorde; lodgings at luxurious Plaza-Athénée; $600 daily per diems but no limousine service. Said fellow, with indescribable tact, instantly accepted.

That would have been a meeting of magnificent minds – but did it ever happen? The *Compendium* will not say. I doubt the Oulipo has more money in its kitty than a single round-trip fare on a commercial airliner. Was this a display of chivalric hospitality never to be taken at face value? Or was Mathews a multi-multi-millionaire?

Equally astonishing is the dinner menu, duly recorded in the minutes. This positively Lucullan feast included Petrossian Sevruga caviar, new potatoes stuffed with foie gras, *canard rouennais au sang*, all accompanied by spectacular wines, among them Château Margaux 1949, Cristal Roederer Champagne 1953 and the greatest Sauternes of all, Château d'Yqem 1947.

Damn the Oulipo! Damn their rigid rules! Why could I have not been made a member for just that one evening? I would have been able to keep my promise to not say a word if somehow, even by conjure, I could have partaken of a banquet possible only in dreams most deliriously-delectable!

Publications

Everything printed under the Oulipo's aegis can be divided in two – *Bibliothèque Oulipienne* (BO) and Collective Publications of the Oulipo (CP). The former is published by the workshop itself, the latter by various small presses, mostly in London and Paris. Longer Oulipian works by individual authors have appeared by grace of publishers around the world.

The BO, inaugurated 1974, comprises a collection of particularly short almost-pamphlets, best called chapbooks, as they contain anywhere from 5 to 50 pages. Each is written by one or a group of Oulipians and contains any of the following: specimens of the myriad restriction-categories; an homage to a no-longer-corporally-present Oulipian; work-structure-, methodology-, procedure-explanations; emendations of anticipatory plagiarists' work making them more "correct." By now the BO numbers some 200 works; new ones appear at a rate of about a dozen per year; the *Compendium* (a CP) gives synopses of each one up to its own publication-date; do not be thrown by BO 666 as its out-of-sequence number was seemingly necessitated by its title, Oulipo, *Diable!* (Oulipo, *the Devil!*)

Every "fascicle" has a press-run of exactly 150 copies, which are sent off to individual subscribers and institutions – save an extra 60 which belong in the preserve of Oulipians. The publisher *Le Castor Astral* is roughly at the half-way mark of anthologizing these rarities. Authors may have their work supported by government funding-agencies, though not the grand Ministry of Culture. Publishing costs are covered by CP royalties as well as other Oulipo activities, to be pursued later.

The CP is a considerably smaller collection of volumes, all of them, however, of distinctly greater girth. The works therein are credited to the Oulipo as a whole or to certain members. They might contain meetings-minutes; a manifesto or two; BO issues or their translations; bits of history with an early one having a particularly enticing section called "Grab-bag" (which includes variations on different plays performed simultaneously).

Georges Perec

I believe the greatest tragedy to ever befall the Oulipo is the premature death, at age 46, of Georges Perec (member since 1967) when he succumbed to lung cancer in 1982. In the space of only fifteen years as member he was not only prolific, his work scampering over a wide spectrum of the Oulipo composition-lexicon, but also possessed of a mind so preternaturally inventive and ingenious as to produce the Oulipo's (possibly) most celebrated creation, *La Vie mode d'emploi* (*Life A User's Manual,* 1978), a novel so rigorous, original and fascinating the august *Le Figaro* felt compelled to call it "the novel of the decade."

As an artist he was so admired, as a person so beloved, an outpouring of homage and affection has continued to this day – in the form of any number of works dedicated to him as well as continuing riffs on his story *Le Voyage d'hiver* (*Winter's Journey*), which over the decades spawned *Le Voyage d'hier* (*Yesterday's Journey*), *Le Voyage d'Hitler, Le Voyage d'Hoover* before metastasizing into *Le Voyage des Verres* (*The Glasses' Journey*), *Le Voyage du Grande Verre* (*The Large Glass's Journey*, a hat-tip also to Duchamp) and *Le Voyage d'H … Ver …* (*The Journey of H[ugo] Ver[nier]*, the imaginary poet around whom this cycle swirls).

Two years after his death most, if not all, Oulipians contributed to *A Georges Perec* (*For Georges Perec*), a singular homage celebrating his artistry in ways referencing his life and/or echoing his own formalistic restraints. One particularly touching offering is the poem *Ce repère, Perec* (*That landmark, Perec*), by Luc Étienne (member since 1970), which serially repeats the title's letters in bold capitals – forming a black rectangle alike a death-notice enclosure – these letters now becoming words' beginning and ending for each line (though not in English translation). The depth of respect, lamentation and reverence permeates its closing lines:

> *For us, like sailors wishing to change course*
> *And searching past the storm-sail for a beacon*
> *There remains a bright memory to guide us*
> *As we turn towards it as towards our Mecca*
> *That landmark, through our tears, is Perec*

* * *

Perec's life began seeped in misfortune: born in Paris (1936) of Polish stock, his father was a World War II casualty when Georges was only four; two years later his mother died in Auschwitz. Relatives raised him in the French Alps and beyond. He pursued studies at the Sorbonne in a haphazard manner, later earning his living as a public-opinion analyst, then as research librarian. Before age 20 he began writing reviews and commentary to literary publications; by 30 he had published his first novel; plays, poetry-collections and more were to follow. Perec co-directed a film based on one of his novels, *Un homme qui dort* (*A Man who Sleeps*) and continued his involvement in that medium. Love of words, however, expressed in myriad ways, was undoubtedly his primary passion – he was even on a weekly's staff alchemizing wicked crossword puzzles.

I must restrain myself from dilating on his peerless expertise in aforementioned Oulipian composition-*délices* but cannot help mentioning a feat concerning palindromes, those texts which read identically both forwards and backwards, a most famous one being – *A man, a plan, a canal – Panama.* In 1969 he constructed a brilliant specimen containing an astounding 5,000-plus characters! The *Compendium* tells us it – *seems unlikely that any work of its kind will soon match Perec's combination of length, ingenuity, and literary elegance.* (David Bellos, Perec's biographer and translator, reports this palindrome, in a handwritten and unsigned version, was handed to French teachers and students to be marked as an essay and for an "exercise of *explication de texte.*" It elicited a wide array of shudders: student's incompetence; an example of surrealist "automatic writing"; the adolescent author is "in a dangerously paranoid state"; wondering if it was "LSD or marijuana that had generated the disconnected images of the text.")

Life's Lives

L *ife A User's Manual* is a colossal 500-page mosaic of hundreds of tales, all plucked from residents' lives, both past and present, all occupying a single Parisian condominium, namely *11 Rue Simon-Crubellier.* (Before rushing to your guidebook to ascertain in which *arrondissement* this edifice is located, please be informed the street exists only in Perec's imagination.) All these stories – from sweet to frightening, gentle to brutal, commonplace to outrageous – are woven into an intricately-textured tapestry of … well, life itself – with all its hopes and despair, frolic and fury, tedium and suspense, pettiness and grandeur.

You will encounter misunderstandings lasting decades and real accidents along with those not perceived as such. Crimes will be committed for multifarious reasons including not resisting seeming-invincibility and providing sexual turn-on. In such a large building it would be impossible to not find tenderness and love – only to have them balanced by tragedy and death, both natural and otherwise.

The worlds of theatre, ballet and circus will permit peeks. Endless artworks and countless books will come to your attention including a memoir wherein numbers of condo-residents are fictionalized. And seeing we are in Paris, emphasis on food and drink is *de rigueur*, including menus of multi-course uni-coloured dinners.

Certain stories you will find plain and ordinary, some will stagger you with their convulsions and still others will seem fantastical yet strangely believable. The longest ones are inevitably told over the course of winding through the volume's pages – but rarely in chronological order as Perec likes narratives to flitter and flutter. You might land upon a tale's *dénouement*, severely encapsulated, as an introduction to the people involved – only to find many pages later the story's beginning and even later its gripping middle, ploughing in considerable detail to that same, suddenly powerful, *dénouement* that so many pages ago held no significance.

Most residents' lives are intertwined – to greater or lesser degrees – moving towards a point where their confluence begins to resemble a large family. It is touching, at times, to see caring's extent for each other. Most realistically, though, not everyone gets along. Of some people you will be granted a mere glimpse whereas others will draw you towards deep understanding. A greedy resident may have "inherited" a perfectionist's apartment; one obsessed may live directly below another overflowing with hubris. In this way no aspect of life seems left untouched – from the calmest sanity to the wildest lunacy and most everything in between.

* * *

In order to understand the novel's premise you must first jog memory and recollect, or envision with photos-aid, one of those magnificent nineteenth-century buildings one sees throughout Paris' famed centre: weather-grayed once-cream-coloured stone; arched entranceway; floors all facing streets with French doors leading to mini-balconies; eaves with cubby-hole-row for servants, nannies and *au pair* girls. You must next dig up sidewalk's pavement and excavate a floor's worth of dirt before – with world's hugest sharpest cleaver in hand – slicing off the entire façade thus exposing all the building's dwellings down to its subterranean cellars. Every apartment's room(s) – along with its occupant(s) – the stairways, lifts and storage-spaces are now ready for examination – and Perec will describe them all in excruciatingly meticulous detail.

* * *

Now that we have our house "in order" as it were, we can move on to *Life*'s methodology and Perec's constraints, of which he has written extensively. Let's start with the (mathematical term) "Græco-Latin bi-square" which is a perfect square filled with equal-sized square boxes, each containing two numbers. So a 6 X 6 bi-square will consist of 36 boxes forming 6 vertical columns and 6 horizontal lines; each column and each line contain two identical number-sets, 1 through 6, in any order – however each of those numbers 1-6 may occur only *once* in each column and each line. This may sound uncomplicated until you realize each box belongs simultaneously to *both* a line and a column. Correctly constructed, the square will contain no box with the same number-pairings.

How does a Græco-Latin bi-square become a literary device? Perec explains this with admirable clarity using a 3 X 3 bi-square (thus 9 boxes) and, with tiny alterations, I copy almost verbatim:

Imagine a 3-chapter story with 3 characters – Jones, Smith and Woods.

Each individual has 2 sets of attributes. First, headgear – a cap (C), hat (H), beret (B). Second, something hand-held – a dog (D), suitcase (S), rose-bouquet (R).

You now set yourself the task of telling a story in which these 6 items will be ascribed to each character in turn, without anyone ever having the same attribute-pairing. Here is a solution –

	Jones	Smith	Woods
chapter 1	CS	BR	HD
chapter 2	BD	HS	CR
chapter 3	HR	CD	BS

So in the first chapter, Jones wears a cap and carries a suitcase; Smith wears a beret and clutches a roses-bouquet; Woods wears a hat and cradles a dog.

In the next chapter, Jones now slaps on a beret and carries a dog in his arms; Smith's head is now hat-covered and is wheeling a suitcase (with handle in hand); Woods now dons a cap and dangles a roses-bouquet.

In the final chapter, Jones' head is adorned with a hat, clasping a roses-bouquet; Smith protects his head with a cap and walks his dog (leash in hand); Woods sports a beret and lugs a suitcase.

All that remains is to invent situations to justify these successive transformations.

Now imagine the intricacies inherent in *11 Rue Simon-Crubellier*: it has 10 floors, each with 10 rooms (or "units" as a staircase is hardly a room). The execution of a 10 X 10 bi-square is so cruelly challenging it was thought, for over 200 years, to be impervious to construction, until 1967 – in the nick of time, as it turns out – when three mathematicians, working together, arrived at a solution.

For *Life*'s purposes, each bi-square vertical column represents all rooms within that axis and each horizontal line ascribes all the given floor's rooms. Each box then becomes a chapter located in a specific room. Once Perec designed the layout – location, resident(s), and rooms-number in each apartment (along with the uninhabited spaces) – he could place his finger on any box and know exactly where he was in the building. Both numbers in each box represent an item, attribute or grouping, for example: red, cat, art book, tea, clocks, posters, 2 persons, appointment books, solid colours, wool, astonishment, occupants, copper, triangle, socks, coal, literary quotation (perhaps altered), indoor plant.

If I understand correctly, Perec made 42 lists of 10 attributes each – for each box to contain 20 discrete "things." These will then go through their permutations which will – *determine the material of each chapter*. He called this list his – *schedule of obligations*. My confusion is caused by Perec stating – *for each chapter, it listed 42 themes that must appear in it*. How can there be 42 themes in each chapter when the two numbers in each box contain a total of 20?

My bewilderment is not difficult to explain. Anyone who has worked with me knows I insist time must be taken to name every element in the clearest way possible so everyone is famil-iarized with this "appellation." Once decided upon, it must never change. This is our "working terminology." How can each of "red, cat, art book, etc." be a "*theme*"? I see them as *materials* in novel's composition, *tools* at narrative's service.

Perec refers to the 3 X 3 bi-square as – *2 series of 3 items*. When he calls the chapters (or is it the characters?) "items" and the dog/hat or hat/roses a "series" I find it confusing. Is it a mis-print? Is the dog/hat/roses a "series" because those things are going through permutations whereas characters and chapters remain unchanging entities? No matter which way you look at it, if you insist on using the terms "series" and "items," it makes much more sense to me to call the chapter-progression a "series" and refer to the dog/hat/roses as "items." So my confusion is compounded when Perec tells me *Life* is – *21 times 2 series of 10 items*. There is no reference to the word "times" when he speaks of the 3 X 3 bi-square. Does that mean "it" happened one "time" and that fact is so obvious as to be unworthy of mention?

I have spent hours trying to figure this out and am still flummoxed! This irritates me as when an author seeks to elucidate a particularly difficult composition-system one would wish for particular clarity and simplicity in its explanation. On the other hand, perhaps I am one of only a pathetic few who finds all this comprehension-challenging. Perhaps this can all be explained by my experiences in senior school where I consistently did poorly or failed math …

No matter what exactly times, series, and items pertain to, I think we can agree that with *Life* we are dealing with a fiendishly elaborate complexity. While within the annals of novel-writing this creation-method may indeed have very few related examples, other recent arts have used analogous techniques, working within self-imposed constructs of similarly-maniacal precision and rigour.

* * *

Oulipians stress the relationship between mathematics and writing yet I have never come across their acknowledgment of any links between word- and music-composition. Stravinsky was one who demanded precise constraints. Working with Balanchine on *Orpheus*, he wanted to know the music's duration he was to compose for a specific *pas de deux*. Balanchine's response – according to Bernard Taper's fine biography – *Oh, about two and a half minutes.* Stravinsky immediately bristled – *Don't say 'about.' There is no such thing as 'about.' Is it two minutes, two minutes and fifteen seconds, two minutes and thirty seconds, or something in between? Give me the exact time, please, and I'll come as close to it as possible.* Apparently it was – *a reproof Balanchine never forgot.*

Significant parallels occur between Perec's approach to *Life* and constraints governing numerous 20th century musical compositions – not to forget *all* classical literature and music have been rules-bound, the difference lying in Oulipians *devising* their own restrictions while past creators have followed their era's *conventions*. In the first paragraph of a chapter "New means of organization" from H. H. Stuckenschmidt's concise overview, *Twentieth Century Music*, he insists – *A state of affairs in which all choices are open – because no laws exist or are acknowledged – militates against artistic creativity.* He goes on to consider the Schoenberg-championed 12-tone scale which topples tonality's tyranny and gives each pitch equal value. The original note-sequence, selected by the composer, may appear in three other guises: inversion (upside-down), retrograde (backwards) and retrograde inversion (backwards upside-down) – thus four possibilities totalling 48 notes. When one wishes to transpose a tone-row, with its full manipulation-complement, to any other of the 11 available notes (of the diatonic scale) then a new 48-note version is at one's disposal. This number is flavoured by allowing any note to jump or drop an octave or three.

Serial techniques, even more densely constrained – *are essentially a systematic transference of Schoenberg's twelve-tone technique to elements of musical sound other than pitch* – namely rhythm, notes' timbre and duration. Many of these bold thrusts happened in France, Olivier Messiaen and Pierre Boulez being prime innovators. Stuckenschmidt goes on to cite some work by the Greek composer Iannis Xenakis whose – *complex linear polyphony collapses into a series of 'statistical' audio-mosaics.* Further on he calls his music "stochastic," a mathematical process, before saying it – *gives little inkling of the complicated probability-calculus techniques that it employs.*

I have just mentioned only a few sparks from the century's musical bonfire but certainly not out of any desire to detract from Perec's pushed-to-the-extremes way of constructing a literary work. I simply felt the need to point out that analogous hyper-complex ways of music-creation have existed pre-*Life* and to express my surprise – considering repeated emphases on the inspirational connection between mathematics and some Oulipian literature – there seems no mention of this in the exhaustive *Compendium*.

* * *

After this brief "musical interlude" I wish to bring you back to *Life* and its curious circulation-system. Now that Perec had established each chapter's location along with its contents-file, there remained only one technical issue to be solved: the order in which to travel from beautiful salon to enticing kitchen-smells to musty basement. "Tedious" to proceed in a sequential fashion, not acceptable to leave the ambulation to whim or chance, Perec turned to the Knight's Tour, a chess exercise whereby the knight – with its quirky, schizoid moves – traverses the entire board, landing on every square yet never more than once. In order to suit this quest for *Life*'s purposes he enlarged the chess-board to accommodate all 100 "rooms" and found the solution – *rather miraculously, by trial and error.* This arrangement also divided *Life* into six sections, the number of times the knight touched all four sides.

Perec called his way of ordering such a mass of detailed elements – and their flow – *a story-writing machine.* I wonder if you think once the "machine's" data have been assembled (e.g. when Jane goes out for a walk she encounters an ex-lover, a girl who owes her money, a tempting pair of pumps in a store-window, an ice cream vendor and rain-threatening clouds) there is nothing much left to do as the story "writes itself." As a creator in numerous disciplines I wish to immediately disabuse you of this notion. A severe "schedule of obligations" may certainly tax your ingenuity – which should be welcomed by any true artist. One might well be grateful the ex-lover, debtor, rain-threat, etc. have already been imposed on you, thus leaving creativity free to focus on much more interesting issues, ones considerably more tantalizing and gripping than a pair of nifty shoes. Such self-imposed obligations, the mannequin upon which to "hang" one's story, may indeed be a gift – one's mind may now focus on how best to etch that amber's innards, how to draw the greatest musicality out of that ballerina's arm, how to seduce the most plaintive filigree out of that oboe.

Stravinsky agrees. In his 1939/40 Charles Eliot Norton lectures at Harvard he elucidated – ... *my freedom will be so much the greater and more meaningful the more narrowly I limit my field of action and the more I surround myself with obstacles. Whatever diminishes constraint diminishes strength. The more constraints one imposes, the more one frees one's self of the chains that shackle the spirit ... and the arbitrariness of the constraint serves only to obtain precision of execution.* Perec himself was more succinct – *I set myself rules in order to be totally free.* So: uniqueness through noose-tightening; freedom through oxygen-deprivation.

"Nothing"

A t *Life*'s core lies the fascinating Percival Bartlebooth, one endowed with phenomenal wealth though utterly lacking ambition and interests, including those commonly associated with men of excessive means: lusts for power, fame, sexual conquests, vintage automobiles, yachts, nights carousing at gaming tables, spectacular art collections or rare wines. Yet underneath this all-encompassing indifference lurked – *a certain idea of perfection.* When pondering what he should do with his young life he finally decided upon a most elegant solution: "nothing." This "nothing," however, had a very special meaning, taking him months to arrive at the clear formulation of a life-plan – encompassing fifty years (1925-75) – that would keep him fully occupied from ages 20 to 70.

Three principles underpinned his decision. He felt there was an aspect of morality in embracing privacy, thus setting out to accomplish heroic feats or break world records would be inappropriate, yet eschewing publicity did not mean his tasks would avoid difficulties and challenges. All activities would follow dictates of preordained logic, nothing left to chance with dates, places and time-allotments carefully plotted out. Finally, his plan was to achieve a purity of aesthetic nullity, a *tabula rasa* winding its way through creation but culminating in its total obliteration.

How was this grand scheme to be realized? The first decade was inscribed to master the art of painting watercolours. The next twenty years were to be consumed by travel throughout the world, from one seaport to another, at the rate of roughly two per month, in order to render them into aquarelles of identical size (65 X 50cm). Each seascape would then be mailed back to *11 Rue Simon-Crubellier* where master-craftsman Gaspard Winckler would fasten it to a thin wooden board before cutting each one into a jigsaw puzzle of exactly 750 pieces. Post return, the seasoned traveller would devote the last two decades piecing together those puzzles, in order of their creation, with two weeks allotted for each one. Once reassembled, each puzzle would be passed on to chemist Morellet (another condo-resident) who would "retexturize" its surface using a microsyringe to squirt fine-powdered gypsum and gelatinous colloid through capillaries following the cuttings' route, thus reagglutinating all paper-threads, rendering both puzzle and watercolour to their all-but-original state. The solidified puzzle would next be transferred to an expert restorer who, with razor's aid, would separate painting from its backing and remove any glue stuck to its reverse side. The "liberated" original would now be ready to be ferried back to its creation-point where, on precisely the 20th anniversary of its painting, it would be dipped in a colour-removing solution. The emergent verging-on-virgin sheet of Whatman art paper – alas tainted by the faintest lines where puzzle-segments once joined – would then be conveyed back to its owner who could never be duped owing to paper's personalized watermark.

"Nothing" indeed! I can't help but feel Bartlebooth's elaborate life-plan resonates with the First World War's aftershock, its ghastly horrors, just like Dadaists expressed themselves in gibberish as actual words meant "nothing," just like much of 20th Century "serious" music is drained of humanity to be replaced by the "nothing" of bewilderment and chaos, just like painting slowly effaced everything clearly depicting or recognizable in daily life, a declivity culminating with Abstract Expressionists' canvases depicting the essence of "nothing." I realize this is a terribly simplistic way of looking at last century's art yet keep sensing for countless people, devastation-permeated, memory-haunted, soul-shattered amidst death-stench, the meaning of life had become just that: "nothing." Any political stance seemed destined to result in futility if not evil. By far the safest, sanest response might be to self-nullify, to self-vanish, to manifest "nothing." Perec himself states the Englishman's – *arbitrarily constrained programme with no purpose outside its own completion* – was conceived – *in the face of the inextricable incoherence of things.*

* * *

Bartlebooth's quest began well enough notwithstanding the obstacle of possessing neither "spontaneous inclination" nor a quiver of natural talent. Ten years of daily lessons with the condo's longest resident of over 55 years, artist Serge Valène, while not culminating in mastery, did forge a steady competence. During this stage's latter half, his devoted all-jobs man, the quaintly-surnamed Smautf, would make all necessary arrangements, from booking hotel rooms and transport tickets to setting up bank accounts and collecting guidebooks outlining the more-or-less-randomly selected destinations' natures and customs.

Each of the 500 ports had its own flavour – miniscule, sprawling, fog-bedecked, left in abeyance, bomb-devastated, naval, perspiring, iced-over – but once arrived, the routine was identical with the first days reserved for ambulation, observation, sketching and choice of the easel's location. Waterscape's executions, always on the day preceding departure, were conducted in great haste, no corrections allowed, with Smautf standing guard with a sizable umbrella to protect the artist from any disturbing natural elements. Once completed, pigments dry, the seascape was wrapped in tissue, eased into a protective envelope, wrapped in construction paper, tied with string, sealed with wax, and affixed with identical address-label, our painter's latest creation then posted to jigsaw-puzzlemaker Winckler's studio. The concomitant Second World War-years did not alter the expedition's itinerary, causing mere whispers of inconvenience.

Puzzlement

Puzzles were of incalculable importance to Perec – otherwise he would not have made his protagonist's existence revolve around them, nor would he have preceded *Life* with a Preamble on the art of cutting them. Moreover I think it fair to suggest the imposition of restrictions on, say, writing a sonnet is very similar to the conception of a puzzle demanding a refined solution. This does raise a question – is jigsaw-puzzle-making a craft or the creation of an art-work? Pre-*Life* I would unhesitatingly have leaned to the former, owing to my total ignorance of puzzle-making. Now I waver.

Perhaps old-fashioned but I think of great art's power to flood with emotion, mystify, delight, bewilder, surprise, perplex, provoke, astonish, haunt, stun, suspend time, rivet my eyes or ears, make my body and mind feel strange sensations. I cannot, however, imagine a jigsaw puzzle affecting me in any of those ways. Besides, a poem begins, at least physically, with a blank sheet of paper before words are penned on it just as a painting does not exist until final brush-strokes appear on once-vacant canvas. That, to me, seems the act of creation. With a jigsaw puzzle the image is already present. All that remains is to saw it into numerous bits and pieces. That sounds like craft rather than creation.

The issue becomes more complicated when one considers creations in all artistic fields involve craft, great art not being possible without its mastery. Does that mean a poor painting is not art? Or is any painting, by definition, art but relatively few ascend to the heights of *true* art? Another factor is the role manipulation plays, how the artist, dare I say "employs his craft" while striving to create specific moods or feelings in the art-experiencer. This is a discussion I must absent myself from, having never set out to induce particular emotions from an audience. Most every person will have touch-points with fellow humans but bubbles inside with far more instances of divergent, even clashing, opinions, beliefs, experiences and personalities. Any attempt on my part to direct their emotions would end only in failure.

Perec would have no truck with my waffling: machine-cut cardboard puzzles are to be disdained whereas hand-sawed wooden versions by brilliant artisans most certainly result in art. He sees the process of cutting demanding high intelligence and foresight with the cutter as dissembler – *The art of jigsaw puzzling begins with wooden puzzles cut by hand, whose maker undertakes to ask himself all the questions the player will have to solve, and, instead of allowing chance to cover his tracks, aims to replace it with cunning, trickery and subterfuge. All the elements occurring in the image to be reassembled ... serve by design as points of departure for trails that lead to false information. The organized, coherent, structured signifying space of the picture is cut up not only into inert, formless elements containing little information or signifying power, but also into falsified elements, carrying false information.* He continues with a perfect example – *two fragments of cornice made to fit each other perfectly when they belong in fact to two quite separate sections of the ceiling.*

So the first-class cutter's job is to mislead, misdirect, to read the assembler's thoughts and remain (at least) one step ahead of the "victim's" mind. This highly skilled precognition resembles psychological warfare – *despite appearances, puzzling is not a solitary game: every move the puzzler makes, the puzzlemaker has made before; every piece the puzzler picks up, and picks up again, and studies and strokes, every combination he tries, and tries a second time, every blunder and every insight, each hope and each discouragement have all been designed, calculated, and decided by the other.*

It turns out jigsaw puzzles' real experience is not one of gazing upon the completed product but rather the mental and emotional upheaval of assemblage – just like a painting's experience is not the staring at it but rather the sensations-registration thereby engendered. And this assemblage-act involves accumulating knowledge of the cutter's trap-laying methods, sifting through his layers of deviousness while uncovering her *style*, one might call it. Perec is very clear on this matter – *it's not the subject of the picture … which makes a puzzle more or less difficult, but the greater or lesser subtlety of the way it has been cut.*

In the end, Perec wins me over – a craftsman of Winckler's Machiavellian skill and ingenuity deserves indeed to be called an artist.

* * *

Prior to departing on his maiden seaport-voyage Bartlebooth auditioned several puzzle-makers before landing on Winckler, ideal because of his youth (age 22) and Mephistophelian puzzle-making acumen. No one was ever to determine the precise contract terms but the about-to-embark seafarer purchased him and his talented miniature-maker wife a condo in, yes, *11 Rue Simon-Crubellier*, where Winckler padded the workshop's door and, Proust-like, lined its walls with cork in order to claim the quiet needed to possess the steadiest hands and focused mind for devilry's execution. While his patron was capturing the seas, Winckler acquired no doubt the finest instruments and materials, before honing his craft even more sharply, developing evermore inscrutable strategies using watercolours painted presumably by his darling Marguerite.

Once the aquarelles began arriving he followed a ritual: place it on an easel facing natural light and have his eyes devour it; next day attach the watercolour to a backing-board with mildly-bluish homemade glue before coating its surface with protective glaze, never forgetting to slide in a fine paper-sheet between board and painting in order to ease the original's eventual removal; for several days examine every detail with a magnifying glass, then imitate Jackson Pollock by stalking around it – *like a panther in its cage*. Once clarity of design had been achieved, replicate the artist's painting-rapidity by drawing cutting lines, improbably enough, with one hand-sweep on extremely thin tracing paper; make a mould of said paper to ensure cutting-precision; then summon all his patience for the actual "dainty" procedure. Sawing completed, each piece needed to be filed with glasspaper and chamois leather before being gently slid into one of the 500 (of course) "absolutely identical" black cardboard boxes, ordered from Madame Fourcade, another resident, no surprise, of *11 Rue Simon-Crubellier.* All that remained was to number the container, note the seaport's locale and creation-date, tie it up with grey ribbons and seal it with wax before strolling over to *Société Generalé* with its most secure of safety-deposit boxes. Winckler always worked alone, never tolerating the slightest disturbance.

* * *

Once returned from surfing seaports Bartlebooth worked without distractions for the first couple of years, puzzle-completions comfortably on schedule with time to spare for entertainments and entertaining, hosting dinners for friends, relatives, travel-acquaintances, with the help of a cook, kitchen maid, laundress, chauffeur, footman, even an odd-jobs fellow to ease Smautf's duties.

Each puzzle was – *a new, unique, and irreplaceable adventure for Bartlebooth* – and every time he would vow to – *proceed methodically and with discipline, not to rush in headlong*; he would not – *let his passion or his dreams or his impatience get the better of him, but would build up his puzzle with Cartesian rigour.* Post opening each box the determined assembler would follow the same routine after easing its contents on his massive rosewood table: separate straight-edged pieces from the rest as they were most likely to form the puzzle's borders; examine all the others from every angle; form clusters of those indicating a telling detail; sort the rest according to colour-groups and their shades.

Exercise of patience was paramount and the – *main problem was to stay neutral, objective, and above all flexible, that is to stay free of preconceptions.* In other words, increased familiarity with certain pieces would seduce his mind into making connections with familiar shapes and images (hat, lobster, alphabet-letters, Italy's heel-outline) which ended up making the puzzler see pieces in ways unhelpful for fitting them into the actual puzzle. What mattered – *was that for as long as he carried on seeing a bird, a bloke [etc.] … he was quite unable to discover how the piece would slot into the others without being, very precisely, reversed, revolved, decentred, desymbolized: in a word,* de-formed. Designing pieces conjuring real-life semblances was a key element of Winckler's obfuscation-strategy.

Another problem, strangely enough, lay in Bartlebooth's clear memory of vistas he'd painted. Though notes and sketches were all destroyed, his intense observation at the time, along with each painting-creation's-recall turned to his disadvantage – and Winckler, almost uncannily, would divine elements most likely to land in memory's depository before proceeding to wreak maximum distortion. The focused devotee – *sought such special signs almost every time* – though placing faith in them would prove unhelpful. For example, he might dredge up the – *red-and-gold splodge* – of a wool-washing woman which Winckler would make disappear as that colour-blur would be – *cut into a multitude of pieces from which the yellow and the red seemed inexplicably absent, drowned, dismembered into those minute overflows, those almost microscopic splashes, those little errors of the brush and rag which the eye absolutely could not see when the painting was looked at in its finished state, but which the puzzle-maker's patient sawstrokes had managed to exploit and exaggerate.*

Do you remember the blue-tinted glue? It would occasionally spread to the inserted sheet's edge which became the puzzle's border. Bartlebooth would utilize this information and if the – *bluish fringes were perfectly continuous … pieces which at first sight would never have been associated with each other … did in fact go well together.* Yet only for the first hundred puzzles or so. When Winckler intuited this perception would become ingrained, he then created booby-traps out of them. This mind-acclimatization followed by its denial proved mere child's play, however – *merely an elementary subterfuge, a limbering-up exercise.* This was reflective of Winckler's approach, one – *aimed to arouse new confusion each time.* Perec states – *the most rigorous methodology, an index of the seven hundred and fifty pieces, the use of computers or of any other scientific or objective system* – would not have been of any assistance. Winckler had, from the start, begun with a holistic view, having – *clearly conceived of the manufacture of these five hundred puzzles as a single entity, as a gigantic five-hundred-piece puzzle of which each piece was a puzzle of seven hundred and fifty pieces, and it was evident that the solution of each of the puzzles called for a different approach, a different cast of mind, a different method, and a different system.*

On trying days, feeling stuck, his mind would descend into – *a kind of torpor, a sort of repetitive boredom, a veiled befuddlement.* Had you been in the dining room, cogitations' arena, you would have heard – *mere muddled muttering, background noises to a wretched madman's obsessive and sterile musings.* Perhaps inevitably – *after hours of such gloomy inertia, sometimes Bartlebooth would suddenly fly into frightful rages.* This man, known to all as the epitome of "British phlegm," sang-froid, courtesy and rectitude would then unleash furor of startling intensity. On one occasion he rent a small marble table in half with a single fist-blow. On another, Smautf had the misfortune of entering with daily breakfast-tray only to see it sent flying with such force the teapot, with the velocity of a tennis serve, shattered overhanging scialytic lamp's thick glass into countless fragments.

This frightfully expensive lighting device bears a moment's study. The lamp itself is massive and so heavy that its weight, in our Englishman's case, needed distribution over the whole room using an arrangement of cords and pulleys. A scialytic lamp is also among the most powerful known to man. It is used in hospitals for operations, known as a surgical lighthead. Prized for shadow-elimination, its "unfaltering" light is available in powers of 3.8 to 5K lux. To give this force's sense, full daylight releases from10 to 25K lux whereas direct sunlight will blind or fry you with anywhere from 32 to100K lux. Converting lux into watts is a most complicated mathematical formula, nor do I know the precise square-footage of Bartlebooth's study but we can be certain the pure light emitted by this herculean apparatus would be sufficient to delineate every colour's possible shade. The teapot-tempest even had a fortunate ending as due to Winckler's glaze no piece was damaged and in clean-up's course he was to arrive at puzzle's solution more rapidly than otherwise.

In utter contrast to irruptions' paroxysms, Bartlebooth could be swaddled in a cocoon of beatitude. Perec limns this not-in-frequent state with such tenderness I feel obliged to quote at some length – … *at the end of such hours of waiting, having gone through every stage of controlled anxiety and exasperation, to reach a kind of ecstasy, a stasis, a sort of utterly oriental stupor, akin, perhaps, to the state archers strive to reach: profound oblivion of body and the target, a mental void, a completely blank, receptive, and flexible mind, an attentiveness that remained total, but which was disengaged from the vicissitudes of being, from the contingent details of the puzzle and its maker's snares. In moments like that Bartlebooth could see without looking how the delicate outlines of the jigsawed wood slotted very precisely into each other, and taking two pieces he had ignored until then or which perhaps he had sworn could not possibly join, he was able to fit them together in one go. This imitation of grace … made Bartlebooth feel as if he had second sight: he could perceive everything, understand everything, he could have seen grass grow, lightning strike a tree, erosion grind down a mountain like a pyramid very gradually worn away by the gentle brushing of a bird's wing: he would juxta-pose the pieces at full speed, without error, espying, beneath all the details and subterfuges intended to obscure them … whole areas would join up, sky and sea would recover their correct locations, tree trunks would turn back into branches, vague birds back into the shadows of seaweed.*

This Zen-like flotation could not, of course, last forever, and our puzzler – *would soon revert to being a sandbag, a lifeless lump chained to his worktable, a blank-eyed subnormal.* Oblivious to hunger, thirst, heat or cold, he would at times exhibit youth's stamina, struggling for forty hours or more without cessation. Yet more evident was his progressive weakening.

Bartlebooth was to slowly withdraw into himself and his puzzles, permitting no disturbances, eating ever-more sparsely, often slumping asleep in his great-uncle's mahogany armchair by the work-table. Guests became an amusement of the past as contact with others was increasingly limited. Half-way through the second decade his deterioration became even more clearly pronounced. Puzzles had taken the upper hand and no matter how many hours devoted to their completion he had fallen markedly behind.

A while after his seventieth birthday the strain on his eyes became undeniable. Headaches led to vision-impairment: solid objects became blurry; clear air acquired the texture of mist; peering through reduced light was not helpful as – *it seemed that things were reduplicating themselves, as if he were constantly drunk.* After a successful double-cataract operation, Bartlebooth was fitted with powerful contact lenses and told never to allow eye-fatigue. Undeterred, he was back at his table in a month.

In the midst of this growingly desperate attempt to recoup lost time, the slowly-crumbling figure was to face an assault of a completely different nature. Perec consumes ten pages detailing a merger between two giant hotel-chains in order to effect, throughout the world, twenty-four complexes of unheard-of luxury, privacy and sophisticated grandeur. Clients could book week-long stays but, without extra cost, might be whisked from one location to another in order to experience marvels piquing their curiosity and pampered sensibilities.

Having registered this enterprise in Puerto Rico for tax-reasons, the directors were obliged to follow its law stating one percent of the overall budget needed to be spent on contemporary art. Eschewing the prosaic commissioning of local artists to produce anodyne trifles to be hung in lobbies and bedrooms, it was decided to procure works of the greatest magnificence, the collection to be installed in one particular location. Swiss art-critic Charles-Albert Beyssandre was hired as curator of this spectacular gallery.

Oh, what money can't buy! Beyssandre calculated the allotted five billion "old" francs would allow the purchase of – *fifty Klees, almost every single Morandi, almost all of Bacon or practically every Magritte, maybe five hundred Dubuffets, a good score of the best Picassos, a hundred or so Staels, almost the entire output of Frank Stella* – etc. (It is unclear to me, though, if all those old francs would pay for the Magrittes *and* Dubuffets *and* Picassos or would the curator need to choose between those painting-packets.)

Within the art-world's cloistered community, no wonder (inaccurate) news of a "formidable patron" quickly spread, fomenting chaos. If Beyssandre seemed to show interest, a painter's canvas-price would "go parabolic" whereas with the critic's apparent disinterest, values would flash-plummet. The pressure became intolerable. Beyssandre soon not only gave up his columns but announced his retirement with full-page ads in former employers' papers, went into seclusion and limited himself to visiting painters in their studios. After two years of being – *smothered in champagne and* foie gras – Beyssandre checked in to a Swiss chalet to contemplate his decision. There he stumbled on an interview with cineaste Rémi Rorschach (yet another *11 Rue Simon-Crubellier* resident) who expressed an interest in making a film of Bartlebooth's exploits. Never having viewed a single original nor studied a reproduction, Beyssandre, quite unaccountably, considering his ostensible acumen, came to an abrupt conclusion – *those very works which their author absolutely wished to destroy would be the most precious jewels in the rarest collection in the world.*

When Bartlebooth's doorbell went unanswered for months, Beyssandre hounded Smautf, offering vast sums while making clear he would not be deterred in acquiring, at minimum, a single watercolour. Bartlebooth was quick to understand his foe's forceful tenacity and exercised the only realistic option available: he enlisted Producer Rorschach, whose television camera-crews went regularly on assignment to strange destinations, one group-member now entrusted with a side-trip to dissolve colours and return with the effaced paper. Seeing as this person, different from mission to mission, was unknown to the artist, he insisted on the process being filmed, the footage of which he would view and immediately destroy.

Meanwhile, Beyssandre would prove as good as his word. He arranged for an (unsuccessful) burglary of the retexturizer's chemistry lab; attempted arson in the restorer's studio meant to deflect attention, allowing for aquarelle's theft, was to no avail, the puzzler having fallen (yet again) behind, thus presenting no exemplar to steal; even the "mysterious car accident" in Turkey, resulting in four crewmen's death, did not result in a "precious jewel's" capture. Henceforth Bartlebooth resolved to return completed puzzles back to their delivery-boxes before having them tossed into an incinerator. Too late. The puzzle destined for obliteration's debut was never completed.

We have reached endgame. Hotel-megamerger's luxury-manufacture-endeavour floundered and dissolved. Beyssandre forever disappeared. Bartlebooth's vision was reduced to a mere chink before it too merged with opacity. His humour, however, did not blacken. With exultation he realized work need not be abandoned; he had not lost the sense of touch – *he could still distinguish shapes.* Upon discovering a fellow-watercolourist, the "chit of a girl" Véronique Altamont – and how could we doubt her residency's location? – would almost daily visit the newly-blind man and slip individual puzzle-pieces into his hand while describing – *in her still, small voice the imperceptible differences of colour between them.*

It is near end-June 1975. By now our disintegrating warrior is bald, of listless expression, not *entirely* without flesh. One hand clutching that heirloom-chair's arm, the other fingering puzzle number 439's last piece, he faces an insurmountable problem. The tiny gap is so like the shape of an X whereas his hand worries a piece with the clear contours of W, not incidentally Perec's favourite letter. The game is over. Bartlebooth dies.

Failure

The Englishman's life ended in failure: 60 boxes remained unopened and some of those assembled were not disposed of in the manner conceived. Tossing cartons of orphaned pieces into *11 Rue Simon-Crubellier*'s incinerator seems such an ignominious finale when compared to the elegance of Bartlebooth (later Smautf) returning watercolours to their painting-sites in order to be blanched to their original whiteness. How strange – and ironic – to say someone failed in his quest for "nothing"! One would think nothing would be easier to achieve than "nothing." Failure here is akin to the inability to arrive at a destination and I can't but hear echoes of Vladimir and Estragon's futile waiting for Godot.

Was Bartlebooth's grand project doomed to failure? And was he responsible for its demise? From a fanatical cataloguer and systemizer it is curious to read Perec considering it – *tiresome to draw up a list of all the contradictions which appeared in Bartlebooth's plan*. He did conclude, however, the greatest success-defier was inadequacy dealing with Winckler's and Beyssandre's "onslaughts."

For my part, I think the art critic's stalking could never have been imagined, thus impossible to prepare for, yet Perec stands on firmer ground when taking his protagonist to hand for developing and then adhering to a poor puzzle-completion strategy. In the early years, three-day puzzle-solutions were not unheard of. He certainly could have conducted assemblages more rapidly instead of sticking to that once-every-two-weeks schedule. This would have been a wise decision considering the (albeit at that time unknown to him) puzzles' mounting difficulties. Would he have considered it a "failure" to complete all puzzles ahead of schedule? Why not deem it a "victory"? Did he fear a gaping void if life held no more puzzles to puzzle over?

I personally fault the grand venture for making no allowances for contingencies. Granted, the World War ended up not denting his endeavour but what if one of his passenger-ships had been torpedoed? Or his "cover story" found so eccentric it only increased the likelihood of him being deemed a spy? The broken bones from an unfortunate car accident, the resultant inconvenience of weeks spent in a hospital would not have disturbed the schedule if earlier puzzles had been completed at a faster clip. He certainly should have foreseen the inevitable infirmities-increase between ages 50 to 70 along with likely-diminishing mental acuity. Had he consulted an opthalmologist after scialytic lamp-purchase, he no doubt would have been told to restrict exposure to such brilliant light for only a few hours per day. Was part of his intelligence dormant while clocking heroic shifts? Under the circumstances it is rather astonishing his eyes held out for as long as they did.

Perec, as narrator, feels Bartlebooth selected 500 as the number of aquarelles to be painted as it was a nice round number, yet logistically it would have been more sensible to follow the calendar's rhythms, thus deciding on 480 seascapes, meaning two per month instead of being obliged to occasionally crowd in a third. And while we are on the topic of symmetry, why did he not decide on the 500 puzzles to be cut each into 500 pieces? This would have resulted in an average piece-size of

6.5 square cm, just big enough to accommodate my thumb-print. A literally blindingly-difficult puzzle would have fallen instead into the category of strenuously challenging. Perec will not pass judgment on the project's feasibility, whether its "internal contradictions" preordained incompletion, yet feeling that if Bartlebooth's sight had remained unimpaired – *perhaps, even then, he would not have managed to reach the end of the implacable adventure to which he had resolved to devote his life.*

* * *

Bartlebooth's dogged "nothing"-pursuit may have consumed a rather large portion of my considerations here; however, this feels commensurate with our core-figure's over-sized role in *Life's* condo. Detailing his taxing route to failure only underscores a current running throughout the collage's construct as Bartlebooth was hardly the only one to fall short of goal's attainment. Valène, the artist hired to instil a watercolourist's competence, had very late in life imagined a painting containing the entire memory-bank of all his years spent at 11 *Rue Simon-Crubellier*. This painting's perspective was to be the building with its façade removed, all rooms, stairwells, cellars exposed, all personages past and present vivified – in other words a pictorial representation identical in scope and conception to the one actually executed by Perec. Unlike the puzzler, the painter was overtaken by death soon after beginning what surely he imagined his *magnum opus*. Those removing his body from the studio would have seen a canvas unmarked save for some charcoal-drawn boxes – *the sketch of a cross-section of a block of flats which no figure, now, would ever come to inhabit.*

Leaving aside other characters' inability to realize aspirations, Perec himself, strange to say, did not manage to complete what

59

he set out to do. A book designed to contain 100 chapters ended up with 99. (I suppose the Epilogue does not count as a "chapter.") The *Compendium*, most enigmatically, tells us – *for this the little girl on page 295* (231 in Bellos' magnificent translation) *is solely responsible.* And indeed, at first we encounter – *A little girl gnawing at the edges of her shortbread cookies* – a cameo Valène intended to include in his masterwork – only to later find out she is actually not a *real* girl but a drawing of one on a biscuit-box lid, and more accurately – *munching the corner of her* petit-beurre. Yet the way in which this creature is responsible for chapter-omission is hardly elucidated.

But no! Weeks after writing these last sentences I clunked, by accident, upon an entry in the *Compendium* which deals with the clinamen, the rule-breaking rule which allows you to stray from restriction-confines. A clinamen may be used *only* when a solution within the constraint is available but for aesthetic reasons you strongly prefer to substitute that solution with something more pleasing. It turns out the nibbled-at biscuit is called a *Lulu*, which can be broken up into *Lu lu* (past participle of "read") – leading me to assume the pre-schooler must have continued her delicate savouring until no delicacy remained. Thus she could be seen as devouring an entire chapter – or you might say since she had already "read" it (twice no less!) she obviated the need to include it in *Life*.

A more elegant – and accurate – explanation of this clinamen, however, accounts for Perec's penchant for homophones (words sounding alike yet possessing different meanings), and will be found in Paul A. Harris' essay "The Invention of Forms." He points out the biscuit-box is *square*, a "*fer-blanc carré*" ("tin-plate square"); homophonically slight stretching results in "*faire un blanc carré*" ("to make a blank square"); since the omitted chapter is apparently located in the furthermost left-hand box of Perec's Graeco-Latin bi-square and since she nibbled at the biscuit's *corner*, her little snack ended up as chapter-digestion and thus its disappearance from *Life*. This is how the Oulipo-brain works – as well as an indication of the fascination and scholarship-fervour this mesmerizingly convoluted puzzle of *Life* has elicited!

As tasty as this clinamen might appear, I am beginning to smell a red herring. It seems particularly strange for Perec to employ this device not to *escape* from a displeasing solution but rather to use it *in service of* a shortcoming.

Harris has found the author freely admit, in an interview, that any constraint-system may well include – *an anti-constraint built into it* – allowing for – *some free play … one needs a clinamen*. We know Perec relished formidable challenges and was peerless at wriggling out of all difficulties – yet in this instance he has used the clinamen to wriggle *into* a difficulty. Thus it would seem this *petit-beurre*-concoction cannot be considered a true clinamen as he has procured it to subvert his own intentions.

I really suspect Perec – and this is pure conjecture – from the start intended to "fail," always wanted *Life*'s grand mission to mirror the shortfalls of Bartlebooth and Valène – and clinamen "false-usage" was a way of masking (or creating) his all-along desire to not attain the 100-chapter mark. If so, why? Failure is, of course, unavoidable, a part of everyone's life, an inexorable condition of humanity. Was the accentuation of failure's essential essence in our existence crucial to convey *Life*'s faithfulness to real life? For some reason I have never forgotten the story of masterful Giacometti showing his work to a studio-guest, shaking his head while presenting each and every sculpture – *Je n'ai pas reussi.* (I have not succeeded.) We also have Beckett's famous – *Ever tried. Ever failed. No matter. Try again. Fail again. Fail better.* I feel confident Beckett did not consider success even a possibility. The point was to attempt a better job of failing.

Another possibility: was Perec instead highlighting failure-efflorescence in *Life* to reflect the disasters and abominations of last century's first half? Or is it conceivable – if comment or analogy was even his intent – those meditations were closer to home, about the failure inherent in defining what the Oulipo and "potential literature" really *are*, the failure inherent in ever hoping to read more than the tiniest fraction of Queneau's *A Hundred Thousand Billion Poems*? Perhaps the ideas of success, failure, completion and incompletion are somehow unhelpful, misguided. Might it be rather more appropriate, instead, to think in terms of pursuits' pleasures? Levin Becker suggests – *the ideal Oulipian reader is … one who would be content to work on a puzzle she has no hope of ever solving.* In the same vein, an early Oulipian apparently claimed: if death was indeed the only escape from self-constructed labyrinths, then searching for the way out is the "true liberation" as in that search lies the certainty of continually feeling alive. And there can be no doubt that for Perec the act of writing under constraints was his most enriching, inspiriting way of "continually feeling alive."

* * *

After all the hours of pondering and ruminating over *Life* I remain deeply conflicted. Strangely enough the book ends up feeling like a fascinating *artifact* instead of a novel, a term I cannot seem to bring myself to call *Life*. In itself this is a curious observation as my trusty Dictionary.com defines an artifact to be, among other things – *any object made by human beings* – before adding – *especially with a view to subsequent use as a book to be read* – (*Life*'s title indicates it to be used as a manual for living).

Harris has noted in his essay this – *manual of life does not represent life; rather it instantiates the real* – meaning it provides – *instances* of *the real*. This seems a prime example of academic hair-splitting which drives me to distraction: doesn't the *representation* of life provide *instances* of it? While reading *Life*, however, I none-theless continually felt myself observing an artifice rather than immersed in full-blooded reality. Perhaps this was engendered by endless room-contents' descriptions; perhaps the *instances* are too discrete, too scattered, to fully interact and thus deprive life of its essential polyphonic *representation*; perhaps the narrator's utter detachment renders him more automaton than human.

Whatever the reason, save for a few particularly extraordinary tales, I was unable to elude simulacrum's ineffable whiff in *Life*. Harris reinforces this sensation – though only when I read him in a way suitable to my purposes – when he avers – *instead of reflecting the world by imitation, Perec manufactures the sense of being real by copying*. Again my conviction strengthens: aca-demics' worth is enhanced in seemingly direct relation to their ability to obfuscate. My dictionary states "imitating" is akin to mirroring, reflecting, mimicking, impersonating and, yes, mak-ing a copy. So wherein lies the difference in Harris' – *reflecting by imitation* – and – *manufacturing by copying*? I really do not know, but if imitation implies activity performed by humans whereas manufacture by copying is done exclusively by (writ-ing?) machines, then my sense of many pages inhabited by simulacra is reaffirmed. I am more than pleased to bid Harris *adieu* as I likely abide by his certainty that by this process Perec has succeeded in – *generating ... an entirely different register of realism in literature*.

"Different register" notwithstanding, *Life* as a whole is utterly lacking in tension, missing an engine to propel it forward. From beginning to end there is no movement, no direction. Things simply happen, one after another. The impression is looking at a Dadaist collage being created in front of one's eyes, bits of materials randomly floating or dropping before being affixed to the canvas. A moment ago, when I hesitated calling *Life* a novel, you might wonder if I am incapable of appreciating anything not telling a story, with momentum carrying it from beginning to conclusion along the lines of, say, Dickens or Stendhal. Well, of course I am capable – however the effect must be compelling, gripping, entrancing, which *Life* certainly is – but only in fits and starts. Therein lies the problem.

Perec's use of the Græco-Latin bi-square is indeed a fabulously original scaffolding to support a novel, yet I fear he has jammed each square with an excess of list-items resulting in (often) thoroughly useless mind-numbing detail-masses. The Altamonts' cellar contains enough provisions to withstand a months-long siege. But do we really need to know every single type of fish, every single variety of fruit, every single selection of vegetable encased in tin? Would it not have sufficed to say they had an enviable wine cellar with a focus on French regions instead of listing vineyard after vineyard after vineyard after vineyard along with favoured German Rieslings, Hungarian tokay, not omitting aperitifs, whiskeys, sweet post-prandials, cognacs, fruit juices and mineral waters (bubbly and still, by the way)? Might it not have sufficiently enhanced our Altamonts-understanding to state they were distinctly "anal" in storing a plethora of household not-exactly-essentials instead of regaling us with all minutiae, including – *bleach products for unblocking wastepipes, supplies of ammonia bleach, sponges, products for polishing floors, cleaning windows, shining brass, untarnishing silver?* Madame de Beaumont's cellar, in contrast, contains nothing edible or potable but rather books, travel-souvenirs, postcards and photographs, particularly of Anne and Béatrice: sitting in a meadow, holding a dog; in party-dresses; arranging flowers; lying in a hammock; playing dress-up with one an Empress, the other a shepherdess – not to forget the "pharmaceutical prospectus" for an "oral protective paste" called Orabase, original document faithfully reproduced, explaining its advantages (antibiotic-free, application-friendly, tissue-protection from irritation, etc.) and instructions for proper use (dab, don't rub, onto the *affected*, but never *infected*, area, etc.) along with tube-weight options. Fascinating.

The "draft inventory" of stuff retrieved from the stairs does not convey any sense of uniqueness or peculiarity to augment my understanding of the residents' nature. The two-dozen-plus items (alarm clock, shoe, slipper, milk bottle) are all bric-a-brac fallen out of anyone's bag or left behind due to sudden remembrance of an errand urgently to be run. Perhaps I should be grateful the list contains only *some – of the things found … over the years.*

Madame Moreau is 83, a crippled, bedridden widow who still runs a successful decorating-and-outfitting-appliances business. This woman of such determination and misfortune has a wonderfully designed suite of exotic rarities, duly described, but Perec seems most interested in zooming in on the spunky entrepreneur's company-wares' catalogue: wallpapering kit and staple gun; electrical airless paint sprayer; 3-way top flight ladder; WM700 deluxe "workmate"; D142 hammer drill, etc. Catalogue's contents consume several pages as every one of the over 20 items is microscoped in unstinting detail with height, width, weight (wherever needed) along with guarantee-durations (always one year). Salivating.

I could have gone on for quite a few more pages but will now stop – in hopes you will at least have been tempted to dash this book against the nearest wall. I am sure some of you will wail – *But Hillar, you're missing the point. All our lives are full of precisely this type of headache-inducing mundanity. It's an inescapable part of life. That's why Perec put it in there.* And I would fully agree with you – but is this what I want to *read*? Is it not intolerable enough my life seems regulated by booklet-sized contracts; audit spreadsheets; answering grants-applications' increasingly inane queries; keeping to-the-penny investment-records; filing endless documents essential for completing our nation's infamously complex income-tax forms? When you next come for dinner will we talk about our lives' curious events and twists, discuss the ballet we saw last week on separate nights, share book-reviews' intriguing new perspectives debunking "received wisdom" of some historical event – or shall we right away dash upstairs and grab that bulging folder with all my operating and instalment manuals and choose which ones to pore over tonight?

Throughout expressing these frustrations and disparagements my mind has been relentlessly spinning back to Melville, an author with whom Perec was intimate as Bartlebooth derives his name's first half from the short story "Bartleby, the Scrivener," the high-principled, fate-struck, laconic copyist. *Moby-Dick* – repeatedly hailed as a masterpiece if not the "Great American Novel" – continually shadows my thoughts as I remember Melville, in his own way, replicating Perec's flaws. Both books encompass similar quests, one desiring to tell us "everything" about a Parisian condo while the other wishes to engulf us with "everything" concerning whaling. And it is precisely that compulsion with imparting "everything" that mars both works.

Moby-Dick rivals *Brothers Karamazov* in its masterfully-measured scene-setting for the Pequod's voyage, captained by Ahab's monomania vortexed into exacting revenge on that dastardly White Whale who, in refusing to be slaughtered, once smashed his ship and scythed half his leg off. Yet once the vessel begins to sail, Melville feels obliged to refute centuries' injustice against all whalers. Directly after introducing us to the ship's fearless mates, ferocious harpoonists and lunatic Captain we swerve to history's early whale-commentators (beginning with the Bible and Aristotle) and entire-book authors (like Scoresby Jr.) before being led into what might as well be an encyclopaedia: page upon page detailing leviathan taxonomy, with each whale's appellation-history, description, nature, commercial value, hunting-grounds, on and on and on. As the fearsome fish was specifically a *Sperm* whale I would understand being introduced to critical aspects of its nature, a page or two concerning its uniqueness – but over ten percent of the text, to this point, suddenly devoted to the most incurably whale-addicted? This is narrative-hijack. Perhaps even more irritating is Melville leaving the impression of being a hands-on expert whereas it has been proven this detail-deluge had been cribbed from various sources – and then compounding the matter by insisting on the essential futility of these descriptions as their precision is not only elusive but unattainable.

Melville recounts a stress-ratcheting wills-force incident secretly told during a gam – a mid-sea social encounter between captains and mates – a story of insubordination and mysteriously-forced flogging-cancellation (later to be echoed by mate Starbuck's opposition to Ahab's intransigence) which, for some inexplicable reason, entices the author to immediately follow by dilating on the general paucity of skilled whale-depictions in drawings, paintings, carvings and sculpture. This continual digression-larding – totalling almost 20 – serves no palpable purpose and is far more dispiriting than narrator Ishmael's early encounter with – *a very large oil-painting so thoroughly be-smoked, and every way defaced* – as to demand repeated studies and inquiries to determine its subject, a scene propelling Melville into prose so bewitching I have been impelled to revisit it regularly over the years.

So much of *Moby-Dick* inundates us with whaling-particulars while a titanic story struggles to emerge. Comfortably in excess of 25 percent of the book floods us with mind-numbing minutiae – blubber-removal's "blanket"-creation; its reduction to oil, then transference to barrels and storage; most-tricky head-detachment from body; physiognomy of brain, spine, tail, head, spout, skin – all of it unnecessary, none impacting the action. Tension relentlessly mounts; prey has finally been sighted; we are fast on its trail. But now listen to what happens: Melville feels this is the perfect time to expatiate on leviathan's skeleton, vertebrae, fossil-usage in landscaping along with listing ship's victuals-and drink-stock (mimicking Perec's cellars-inventories, though blessedly in less despair-inducing detail). Foreplay *interruptus*.

I will desist and attempt condensation: there was no need for Melville to tarnish his immensely powerful story with needless amplifications on most every aspect of the world's largest mammal. Ahab's obsession suffices; we did not need Melville's. Pages could well have been reduced to paragraphs, even sentences, and thus we might have been enticed, wishing to know more – instead of being swamped, our interest-engine repeatedly grinding to a halt, needing considerable time to warm up again.

Information-impartment could have occurred in increments when apposite to action – instead of vast data-vats arbitrarily dumped over us, cleaving narrative into disconnected chunks.

This submersion in dullness, feeling force-fed the tedious, anaesthetizes the mind. And the brain, once brained, is no longer receptive to *Moby-Dick*'s extraordinary passages, Shakespearean in breadth: akin to the Pequod's ocean-traversions from North Atlantic to South Pacific – with soul-soundings at the greatest depths where our valorous antagonist feasts on giant squids – all amidst sublime evocations of implacable, ever-mutating sea-tempers. These glories I was able to hook only now by side-stepping sideshow-saturation as twenty years ago, in an attempt to "educate" myself, I was at pains to imbibe every word, pleasure evaporating, disgust growing, incredulity mounting: *this is literature considered classic?*

With *Life* as well I have learned what to savour and what to dismiss. Beyond the just-enumerated lists and catalogues we encounter a seemingly-endless number of art-works, all described in careful, caring, detail. To state the obvious: paintings are meant to be looked at. Writing about them can be as problematic as assigning words to illuminate a string quartet. I do not mind making the effort to conjure the appearance of a couple of canvases – but when they mount into dozens my eyes simply glaze over, interest replaced with weariness.

In his postscript Perec lists some thirty authors – most of them well known – from whose works he has smuggled in quotations, permitting himself the occasional minor alteration. Though having dipped into a number of these authors' works I never recognized a single quote. I thought this was testimony to my literary ignorance until finding Harris refer to Sydney Lévy

– a short history of Perec criticism will confirm that only the most knowledgeable specialist of the author quoted will recognize them [the quotes]. These elements go unnoticed because ... they are trivial, insignificant ... [and] play no role in the deployment of any of the numerous plots in the novel ...

How disappointing. I fully concur with Lévy these little pilferings might have formed "the most delectable category" of the "schedule of obligations" – particularly as its *other* obligations completely evade our notice, unless one is devoted to being on sharpest lookout. I am not suggesting the most obvious larceny ("to thine own self be true") but what recognition pleasure-jolts we could have received had Perec secreted fragments imparting the unique flavour or peculiarity of a given work or author – instead of bland phrases capable of being written by most anyone. Incidentally, somewhere in these contemplations I slapped in a sentence from *Lolita*. All I did was change the tense from past to present. Didn't you just *feel* how that little Nabokov-touch enhanced my text?

* * *

After pages of crankiness it is time to touch on some wonders found in *Life*'s glittering kaleidoscope. A while ago I suggested "*Life* as a whole is utterly lacking in tension"; however, this cannot be said about numerous stories therein. Some are entrancing whereas others are deeply moving, mesmerizing, agonizing in the stress they generate.

How gripped am I by the predicament Madame de Beaumont's daughter fell into, the relentless suffering induced, the means employed to extricate herself? So acutely did I feel the need to share those convulsions that five years ago I invited two friends for dinner, preceding it with a little seminar on the Oulipo and following it by reading them that particularly long chapter. Moments ago I called one of them to ask if she remembered – *Of course, it was a most incredible story.* I prodded – *So what do you remember, I mean can you tell me details?* For five minutes I listened to her relating the whole outline, interrupting only twice when her recall was not absolutely perfect. For someone to describe a story's arc with such accuracy, upon a single encounter with years' interval, strongly signals its haunting power.

"The Tale of the Saddler, his Sister and her Mate" seems hardly enticing – but, then again, one should not judge a story by its title. This tale has but the most tenuous connection with crafting fine contrivances for posterior-placement. Instead of dealing with horses we follow the exploits of a master cycler and no matter how great your sports-disdain I defy you to not be dazzled by this improbable, extraordinary sequence of hair-raisers. In fact, while writing this, I resolved to invite the same guest again for dinner – for the sheer pleasure of watching her awe-spasms while listening to this astonishing invention. (I did; she much liked it, eyes dilating in amazement.)

The prospect of reading "Lift Machinery, 2" also does not engender great appetite. It is difficult to imagine much beguilement in ropes, chains and pulleys – yet it contains *Life*'s most spectacular writing. The entire chapter is an anomaly. At the book's end one finds the condo's layout-sketch providing us with each resident's quarters-size and location; the lift machinery is drawn on the same level as cellars and boiler room. Yet, for the first and only time, Perec indulges his imagination in a strikingly different manner as he sees the entire building, from roof to basement, as an iceberg's visible tip while lift machinery's – *submerged mass began below the first level of cellars.* We seem to enter by descending – *stairs with resounding steps going down in spirals* – to the first level which contains, among much else – *long tiled corridors … iron doors stencilled with warnings and skulls … air vents equipped with huge, motionless fans … metal-lined canvas fire hoses as thick as tree trunks … cylindrical wells drilled into solid rock … concrete tunnels capped with regularly spaced skylights of frosted glass.*

We descend to the next level where we hear – *a gasping of machinery, in depths momentarily glimmering with red light* – in – *subterranean halls high as cathedrals* – containing – *men clad in asbestos, their faces shielded by trapezial visors.* The descent continues, level after level after level. For once I cannot complain about pages of lists: the vast expanses' contents and activities within are so fantastical; creatures' working and living conditions grow more and more insupportably miserable, disgusting, appalling; the atmosphere increasingly mephitic, revolting, horrifying. We have entered Perec's *Inferno*. Excoriating. Unforgettable.

* * *

Despite devoting all these pages to *Life* – many more than ever intended for an introduction to the Oulipo Challenge – there remains a great deal unsaid. This is due to its complexities being so intricate, often invisible, as to take perhaps a full year's sustained study to master its Byzantine constructs, fully plumb its depths and solve its myriad puzzles. Another factor lies in my personal shortcomings. I don't think I will ever be able to comprehend certain key elements – despite coming across repeated mentions during my readings and research – for example the notion everything in the book occurs simultaneously as, in Levin Becker's words – *time is suspended for the duration of the book's 500 pages.* I believe the idea is this: since in *Life* we are "reading" the *finished* painting Valène conceived but barely started, then we are seeing everything happen all at the same time – despite following the decades-long process of Bartlebooth's watercolour-travels ending with completed puzzles and their serial effacement. Yet time "suspended"? It is simply beyond my comprehension.

I will conclude by acknowledging the incredible praise *Life* has justly garnered – for its ingenious conception; its magnificent multi-layered construction; its agile manoeuvrings within impossibly rigorous restrictions – yet for me most crucial is the final product. Despite the numerous glorious passages, this feat of writing – which consumed Perec for nine years – in the end swims excessively in a sea of wearying volubility, depriving me of pleasure over too many extended stretches. The extravagant permutating "schedule of obligations" may have liberated Perec as a writer – but its effect on me, alas, was to slowly smother my spirit. No matter how painstakingly Perec describes rooms' contents they lack any personal connection to the reader and thus remain a stupefying array of mere objects: inert, lifeless, lacking humanity. I realize what a terrible thing this is to say of a work meant to be all about life. Please know how much it pains me to say it. If only *Life*'s reading-joys would have been commensurate to the grandeur of Perec's vision!

And now is also the time to surmount my ill-considered reluctance to call *Life* a novel. For too long its artifice kept getting in the way of my surrendering to what it was trying to be. So, of course *Life* is a novel, in fact a most *novel* novel. Alas, it's just I do not find it a *great* novel.

Disavowal

elling a novelist to write one without ever using a particular vowel is akin to asking a pianist to perform a Beethoven sonata without use of a particular finger. Even the most accomplished musician will tell you – *It can't be done!* Yet Perec was not only able to accomplish this stupendous transcendence with *La Disparition* (*A Void*, 1969) but the suppressed letter in question was E, the most frequently used symbol in the French language. This epic lipogram of almost 300 pages, billed as "a metaphysical whodunit," is a *tour de force* equalled by Gilbert Adair who translated the work without also ever resorting to the eschewed letter – though Perec could at least choose his words whereas Adair was obliged to navigate within those choices.

A Void begins with a scene-setting introduction – Paris in anarchic chaos, its residents volatile and starving – the most sensational writing in the whole book. We soon meet the crazed delirious insomniac Anton Vowl (!) who has spent endless days and nights writing, among other things, a diary which concludes with an enigmatic postscript to his friends. He then vanishes. Those close to him, upon registering Vowl's disappearance, begin a search focusing on that postscript in hopes it will yield clues to his present presence, presuming he is still alive. From this point on I can say no more about the impossibly complex plot as it veers and swerves at such high speed and is convoluted beyond my comprehension.

This novel has fun (no chapter 5), is continually self-referential – the unwelcome E is critical to the plot itself – and falls comfortably into the category of "post-modern" before the word was even invented. I find it strange to hear many will not read this book once they find out about the banished E because, ostensibly, they "get it." Actually much pleasure may be derived from diving in – not to solve the mystery but rather to suffer the intoxicating pleasure of language-manipulation. One becomes so conscious of "illegal" phrases the translator would effortlessly have used (if only he could have) followed by gleeful delight when the translator squirms his way into ingenious solutions. Much more than a thriller, *A Void* is a thrilling romp through a linguistic minefield.

Olivier put me in touch with "punk" Monk as soon as I found out he *also* had translated this novel. His version has never been published – apparently he submitted it mere weeks after a contract had been signed with Adair. Ian wrote me a lovely note and included a review – E-less, of course – which had appeared in his book *Writings for the Oulipo* (2005). He has some rather harsh bones to pick, starting with the title which he considers "a clumsy pun" – and with very good reason as the literal translation of *La Disparition* is *The Disappearance* and a void occurs only once the thing in question has actually disappeared. (Ian's more apt title is *The Vanishing*.)

He also takes strong issue with Adair's needless embellishments and finds – *so many additions, omissions and just plain mistranslations that [he] soon had to stop counting*. One egregious example lies in the handling of that cryptic one-sentence postscript. The original text, crucially, includes the alphabet's every letter save E; Adair's version elides four *other* letters thus destroying the essence of the clue and making the line – *void of any point*.

Ian immediately provides a more succinct and "correct" translation. (Incidentally, he feels writing a lipogram missing only one letter – *not, in fact, that hard* – and – *anybody with an inch of wit can do it.* Good luck!)

To Ian's mind Adair has failed in – *fully grasping what his task should consist of [as] a lipogram should not sink to mere avoidance of the given letter.* He feels the – *author ought to find in this constraint a fillip to his imagination … [that] should signify, for a lipogramatic translator, an ability to find a way of saying what his original says, without addition or omission, in so far as his idiom allows him so to do. … [Adair's] translation totally fails to do this.* Despite the significant caveats, he nevertheless has the grace, quite correctly, to find Adair – *witty, and a good wordsmith* – and his version – *an amusing work in its own right.*

Christian Bök

*The text makes a Sisyphean spectacle of its labour, wilfully
crippling its language in order to show that, even under such
improbable conditions of duress, language can still express an
uncanny, if not sublime, thought.*
—from *Eunoia*'s afterword

* * *

Canadian Christian Book, born 1966, at one point changed
his surname to Bök, a slightly bewildering move as his
surname's pronunciation is unaltered. He received a Ph.D. in
English Literature from Toronto's York University in the early
1990s. Shortly thereafter he published *Crystallography – a pata-
physical encyclopedia that misreads the language of poetics through
the conceits of geology.*

Bök spent the next seven years writing the extraordinary *Eunoia*
(2001) which won the grand and prestigious Griffin Poetry
Prize the year following.

Eunoia means "beautiful thinking" and is the shortest English
word containing all five vowels. It is a fierce Oulipian work
of coruscating beauty, intelligence and ingenuity. *Eunoia* is a
"univocal lipogram," a constraint demanding, in this case, the
exclusive use of one vowel throughout each of its five chapters.

Thus the first one consumes A, the second E, etc. Through necessity – as Bök exhausts over 98 percent of the available vocabulary – the most common-vowel chapters (A, E) contain 19 poems each whereas the lesser-used ones (I, U) contain a mere 11 and 5 respectively. Each poem forms a squat rectangle of words; each chapter contains only equal-length lines (E-11, O-13); each line contains an average of ten words; the entire work is exquisitely printed by Coach House Press with more creamy-white than black on all its 82 pages.

Further self-imposed restraints shackle the poet: all chapters must contain at least one entire poem devoted to the craft of writing; a multi-course feast; sex-fuelled shenanigans; a sea-trip as well as a nature scene. Foreign languages may be mined; umlauts and accents are allowed; apostrophes may only denote possession and may never represent vowels (kiss'd, wash'd) as that would be *wrong*: "cheating", making life easier, resulting in an "impure" lipogram. Rhymes occur internally, not at line-endings – *through the use of syntactical parallelism*. Each chapter is dedicated to an art-creator whose name itself is a lipogram – Hans Arp, René Crevel, Dick Higgins, Yoko Ono, Zhu Yu. Bök would ideally have never repeated a single word but failed in this quest as repetitions abound. I do not fault him for these "flaws" as they contribute to the poems' rhythm and musicality. Perhaps as recompense for this shortcoming he forced himself to eschew the letter Y throughout.

Bök bookends his book with "Emended Excess," a six-poem lipogram in E (bringing the E total to 25), wherein he – *exhausts vocabulary unsuitable for use in the retelling of the Iliad* – which makes sense as Chapter E's central character is Helen of Troy. This "coda" is dedicated to Georges Perec – which also makes sense as, after completing his E-less *A Void*, Perec went on to write *Les Revenentes* (*The Exeter Text: Jewels, Secrets, Sex,* 1972), a distinctly shorter work where the E's, after prolonged cruel deprivation, finally get their revenge: no other vowels "invited to the party."

To give you a clearer sense of the aesthetics' singular beauty, here is the first poem from Chapter E:

> Enfettered, these sentences repress free speech. The text deletes selected letters. We see the revered exegete reject metred verse: the sestet, the tercet – even *les scènes élevées en grec.* He rebels. He sets new precedents. He lets cleverness exceed decent levels. He eschews the esteemed genres, the expected themes – even *les belles letters en vers.* He prefers the perverse French esthetes: Verne, Péret, Genet, Perec – hence, he pens fervent screeds, then enters the street, where he sells these letterpress newsletters, three cents per sheet. He engenders perfect newness wherever we need fresh terms.

* * *

Eunoia has a middle, attenuated section called *Oiseau* (yes, the shortest French word containing all five vowels), beginning with a sonnet by Arthur Rimbaud, "Voyelles" ("Vowels"), which assigns a colour to all five. Bök translates this poem freely and composes others dedicated to language-terminology ("Vocables," "Phonemes") before producing "AIEOU," a sonnet-form sound-poem containing only vowels. We then move on to "And Sometimes," which – *itemizes every English word that contains only consonants*: Y figures predominantly here, its I- and E-like sound (think "gypsy," "syzygy") being probably the *real* reason behind its defenestration from *Eunoia.* Just when you think all possibilities exhausted we find an *hommage* to the late "concrete" poet bpNichol's favourite letter, H, a "visual sonnet," its only-H use forming a row of Siamese-twin ladders, some with missing rungs and sidepieces. Certain *Oiseau* works appear in the original, others in the 2009 "upgraded" version.

The postscript immediately credits the Oulipo's – *extreme formalistic constraints* – for inspiring *Eunoia* before specifying the earlier-noted restraints invented for Chapters A thorough U. Bök continues by commenting on each of the other compositions, wherefrom my quotes derive, before acknowledging – *the devoted support of many patient friends*. Yet most puzzling is the afterword's title, "The New Ennui" – a direct reference to front-page's dedication – *for the new ennui in you* – bolstered, but adding only to bewilderment, by Coach House co-editor Darren Wershler's quote – *"The tedium is the message."* Are we having a bit of fun "channelling" Marshall McLuhan? How a work that held me in such thrall could have delivered either "ennui" or "tedium" can be explained only by this book's perusal by the misguided, the pounced-upon, the conned.

Though *Eunoia* throughout is a staggering, stupefying linguistic marvel, I find the collection's core, Chapters A-U, the most beguiling, rapturous:

Bard's craft all a class act: grammar attracts, charms and grants gasps – a phantasm! Aah! Brava! Aah Allah!

He excels – never nettles, never delves pell-mell – he reveres excellent decrees. These texts present clever sentences, new metre, free verse, pre-fettered speech – even perverse cheek! He expresses perfect freshness-sprees. He engenders senses freed.

His wild writing whirls with skill, sings with vivid skirling chic, winning wit. This writing swings!

Horrors! Bök's bold book holds no comfort-cocoons! Worn mono-chord? Oh, no. Color-blobs glow, throb! Bök's book molds word-rooms of gold! Bök's words morph old word-worlds, show off lots of hot know-how! Go now, swoon!

Gulp! Such much fun stuff stuns plus churns up such lust — must clutch, must suck, must fuck!

* * *

Over the past decade Bök has embarked on a rigorous and astounding poetic quest, one that struck me as having nothing to do with the Oulipo – until I found out Le Lionnais, in a manifesto, had compared the group's formal inquiries with – *attempts to synthesize life artificially.* Only to intensify the connection, I became aware that three Oulipians of mathematical bent (Jacques Bens, Claude Berge and Paul Braffort, members since 1960, 1960, 1961) had once mused – in response to John Conway's breakthrough "Game of Life" computer programme, called a "simulation game" due to its rules simulating real life processes – about the possibility of – *cellular prosody.*

Leaving Toronto, Bök entered University of Calgary to study gen-etic engineering in hopes of creating "living poetry," a life-form capable of not only storing a poem but responding to it with its *own* poem. After first proving the venture's viability in a colony of E. coli bacteria, Bök is now apparently on the cusp of (or has already succeeded) implanting the genome of an "unkillable" bacterium with a poem. This genome ostensibly has the capacity to not only "read" this poem but respond by "manufacturing" a protein, the amino-acids-sequence of which will "encipher" its own poem. (My language is so guarded and phrases cribbed as the process described is incomprehensible to me.)

Book I of *The Xenotext* (2015, Coach House) spent about half an hour in my hands. It contains poems, texts and illustrations leagues beyond even a glimmer of understanding on my part. I believe it's the editor who has called it – *a kind of 'demonic grimoire' … a Virgilian welcome to the Inferno … the 'orphic' volume in a diptych, addressing the pastoral heritage of poets, who have sought to supplant nature in both beauty and terror.* Book II intends to document this creation-experience, one that for once bears the true meaning of "artistic experiment."

With *Xenotext* Bök has given us new meaning to "immortality." No matter which manner humanity decides to obliterate itself, his genome-poems – and those of his "companions" – may well outlast the glories of Homer, Sappho, Shakespeare and Eliot.

Today 2018

During its first decade the Oulipo was essentially forging its foundation: figuring out what it was, what it stood for, what its aims were and how it intended to execute its goals. This was a time when very few knew of the workshop's existence. The second decade was one of consolidation towards the end of which any notion of clandestinity – at least in France – was shattered by the publication of Perec's *Life* and the extravagant laurels accorded it. Since that time the Oulipo has become something of an institution with its own bank account and recognition as a legal entity, an "association" which surely lies outside the domain of commercial enterprises and likely gives it tax-breaks of some kind or another.

Much has changed and much has not: monthly meetings are still held, BO publications continue apace, members give up the ghost and new ones are "co-opted." The Oulipo, however, has acquired a continually increasing public face extending from Paris to throughout France and well beyond.

Since 1996, public readings of texts both old and new occur once a month, October through June, on a Thursday (*les jeudis de l'Oulipo*). At the *Bibliothèque nationale de France* (BNF, Mitterrand branch) a handful of Oulipians and perhaps a guest will perform for a loyal band of devotees; the 425-seat auditorium may be packed, necessitating TV screens to accommodate overflow; proceedings are informal; guessing-games involve the audience and end up being crowd-pleasing if not hilarity-generating. BNF donates the space; no admission charged; chapbooks are sold; audience-members may mingle post-performance with the un-paid Oulipians who soon leave to board the *métro*, just a station, sweetly enough, from the one named in honour of Queneau.

This new-found popularity has not been without reservations as Levin Becker notes the – *difference between traditional oulipian work and what has become to be known within the group, medium-smirkingly, as Oulipo light*. The audience-participation elements are – *short on literary gravitas [yet] delight a crowd all but guaranteed to appreciate it*. The concern: public success has caused the Oulipo – *to shift its energy more toward performance, and to tailor more and more of its texts for a listenership rather than a readership*. Some venerable Oulipians are not exactly thrilled that, as President Fournel (member since 1971) explained – some people – indeed, most people – *are interested in the Oulipo as a performing group: they have been coming to readings for years and years but have never read a printed oulipian line*. Those members fear response to literary market's – *demands for people and not printed matter* – will morph a *société de littérature* into a *société de spectacle*. Fournel bemoans the gruelling overseas and continent-spanning performance-itineraries – unaccompanied by requests for hard copies of writings.

Those who fret over the "lightness"-preponderance might take solace in numerous text-heavy workshops the Oulipo has been invited to give, since 1976, throughout France – whether in Lille (Monk's former home), small-town Pirou (Normandy) or public schools where, curiously enough, the very young students manage particularly delightful Oulipian gurgitations. The most intense course occurs in Bourges, a small town nestled in France's centre, where for a decade some 50 people have gathered for an annual week-long version of Oulipo's "boot-camp." These aficionados – we might call them "groupies" as many regularly attend *les jeudis* and outside-Paris seminars – are mentored in small groups by a half-dozen Oulipians. For the first two days everyone used to be immersed in identical restriction-modes – whereas now all are divided into different specialized groups from the start.

The experience sounds most convivial: everyone receives personal guidance in texts they are struggling with; the mentor-apprentice ratio is ideal; the art-school courtyard is charming; the atmosphere fosters camaraderie as frustrations and moments of *eureka* are shared. Every evening one or two Oulipians give a reading to which the entire town is invited. The grand finale is a recital by all attendees. Levin Becker remembers how the – *Oulipians lurk at the sides like stage mothers while the performers radiate excitement, sheer jittery satisfaction at getting to share their literary mischief.* After all those exertions, how rewarding and thrilling it must be to frolic and flirt at the moonlight-picnic amidst icons and fellow-conspirators, all quenching thirsts with no-doubt-liberal quantities of Mènetou Salon wine! Yet solace is not to be granted to everyone. Even back in 2001 Fournel wrote such events were propelled by outside forces, not initiated by the group itself, and even though several members have pedagogical experience, the desire – *was middling, and even today certain Oulipians are, frankly, hostile towards courses and workshops.*

* * *

This section began with a suggestion the Oulipo, at one point, became something resembling an institution. The appearance of *La littérature potentielle* (1973) was a true foundation-stone seeing as it was brought out by the most estimable *Gallimard* and contained not only Le Lionnais' two manifestos but early restriction-principles' dictates and usage. The first *Bibliothèque Oulipienne* publications began a year later, although reaching the tiniest readership. Perec's *Life* (1978) as well as Calvino's *If on a Winter's Night a Traveler* (1979) caused commotions: theory had been put into serious practice; *potential* literature had become *actual* literature. *Gallimard* followed up with *Atlas de littérature potentielle* (1981), an amplification of Oulipian practices while revealing its first forays into computer-assistance. It was not until 1998, however, with the *Compendium*'s publication, that the Oulipo's foundation became complete and rock-solid. Not only had the workshop's accomplishments' breadth become so extensive as to fill a sizable tome but it marked the first major English publication, greatly widening the Oulipo's readership while carrying the prestigious imprimatur of both the Arts Council of England and the French Ministry for Foreign Affairs.

A foundation so secure begs edifice-erection. And so it was, 30 years to the day of Queneau's death, Oulipians gathered at the *Bibliothèque d'Arsenal* (a BNF-branch), Champagne glasses in hand, to celebrate the first step in a public archive-creation. Granted, this "edifice" is not a building unto itself; granted the library allocated an office-size room insufficiently sizable to accommodate all members-plus present as some were obliged to bask in the adjoining room, appropriately enough, dedicated to Perec's papers. Nevertheless, for a nation-defining library to recognize a literary movement's significance by dedicating a niche for its endeavours' posterity-preservation is a signal confirmation of its institution-status. The Oulipo has indeed come a long way from being just a miniscule animated clique of like-minded wine-loving curiosity-besotted literature-inquisitors.

It must have been quite a relief for Oulipians to divest themselves of cartons full of manuscripts, notes, drafts, journals, books, press clippings, meeting-minutes and Levin Becker, pre-investiture, became the sought-after *esclave* (slave) who for months would sort through and organize the posters, photographs, financial statements and diverse memorabilia. Of particular interest was the correspondence – fan-letters, amateur constraint-offerings mixed in with some really striking writing, alas accompanied by the fatal request for membership-consideration. One Oulipian requested her name's deletion from the ranks. If not ready for euthanasia, I'm not sure why she even bothered.

A 2001 missive laid out, for the next meeting, questions dealing with the Oulipo's future and Levin Becker feels it was – *curiously appropriate that the big questions ... are no closer to being resolved than they were in 1960.* All those minutes charting the group's evolution are so "precious" since they provide – *the instructive value of self-rereading*; the archive serves as a centralized – *access to its origins*; the history is so important for the members because one never knows which constraint, in abeyance for decades, may suddenly spark a new variation, an unexpected twist. One must remember the Oulipo is not dissimilar to the ouroboros – if not actually devouring its own tail then never forgetting its self-nourishment potential.

* * *

A completely different branch of "Oulipo-institutionalization" concerns fathering a whole series of off-shoots wishing to apply Oulipian techniques – or create new ones – apposite to their artistic discipline. Le Lionnais opened the door in 1973 by coining *Ou-*x*-po*, acronym for *Ouvroir de* x *Potentielle* (Workshop for Potential *x*) and went on to found the *Ouvroir de*

Littérature Policière Potentielle (Oulipopo, concerning detective stories). He then continued, over the years, to midwife many new workshop-adventures: comic strips (Oubapo); music (Oumupo); photography (Ouphopo); tragicomedy (Outrapo); painting (Oupeinpo), etc.

Since the early 1990s these offsprings have been proliferating at a rate of one per year. You must not expect, however, to find a lengthy catalogue of filaments radiating from the Oulipo's core: some flourish to this day while others have dispersed or evaporated, just like my own company's (DNA Theatre) decade-spanning, though unsanctioned, addition in the field of ballet (Oubalpo).

Digging Deeper

If this piece has piqued your interest then, of course, the thing to do is dive into some of the group's writing. This is a trifle easier said than done as you can't just pick up a book by an Oulipo-member and presume it is written with restrictions or following certain mathematical principles. Oulipians write whatever they wish to; their work can be divided into non-, quasi- and pure-Oulipian. Mathews' *oeuvre*, for example, contains only one truly Oulipian novel, the strangely off-kilter *Cigarettes* (1987). Then there are clearly Oulipian works written by non-members (like Bök's *Eunoia*). Wishing instead to probe the workshop itself, you would be best off to spend time with the two works, very different from each other, I have been consulting throughout in order to whet your appetite with as much accuracy as possible.

The *Compendium* has a marvellous introduction distilling the Oulipo's genesis, history and intentions. You will also find biographies of all members (until 2005) along with overviews of their work and each one's particular significance to the enterprise. All those constraints – and many dozens more – I have been attempting to tantalize you with (asphyxiation!) will be elucidated and you will often be presented with concrete examples, thus allowing you to see, for example, what a prisoner's restriction actually looks like. You will find out which works are strictly Oulipian; you will discover non-members' work adhering to constraints; you will meet "anticipatory plagiarists" along with snippets of all these writers' texts. Those with mathematical leanings will, unlike myself, understand the usage of Fibonacci number sequences, game theory, graph systems and combinatorics. You will be informed of every *Bibliothèque Oulipienne* issue (again until 2005) with occasional selections. The book ends with a section on the Oulipo's offshoots (like Oumupo). The *Compendium*, with all its alphabetical entries, is user-friendly and to be taken as an indispensable reference book.

Levin Becker's *Many Subtle Channels*, in contrast, is meant to be read from beginning to end, logical chronology-shifts notwithstanding. This is a highly rich personal memoir detailing how he became attracted in the first place; how he followed this up with a stint in Paris immersing himself in all things Oulipian; then becoming a member himself and what that feels like and means to him. Alive Oulipians cease to be who's-who dictionary-entries and spring to life – Levin Becker reveals a sense of their personalities, beliefs and quirks. Instead of *corpus*-overviews he selects certain examples and dilates, sharing his own assessments that result in occasional mini-reviews. Seeing as it is more recent than the *Compendium*, you will be introduced to the newest Oulipians as well as the latest restriction-innovations (baobab; *opossums célèbres*). He limns the Oulipo's evolution before dealing with present-day concerns and challenges. He presents both sides of the complicated, most vexing issue of whether or not works' constraints should be revealed. Levin Becker's style, brimming with brio, sparkles with wit, fades into contemplation, and is always direct, making you feel he is sitting across the table talking only to you.

All That Is Evident Is Suspect: Readings from the Oulipo 1963-2018 is an entirely different beast. The title's first part is a phrase used in an intense inquisition by Jacques Duchateau (member since 1960), a meditation on how structure, mathematics, machines and science might be (or are) related to literature. Edited by Monk and Levin Becker, published in late 2018, the title's second part is exactly what it suggests – a rich overview of the Oulipo's evolution as expressed in thought and practice. Every member is represented by at least a snippet of their work, all in roughly chronological order of composition, favouring those least heralded over the internationally renowned. The spectrum is particularly wide, embracing theory, explication, meeting-minutes but mostly examples of ingeniously fettered Oulipians in action with their fertile minds and pens. Each excerpt or complete work is accompanied by a brief, always illuminating, note concerning perhaps the author, the text's nature, the circumstances of its writing. The range is staggering: you will encounter most implacably serious brain-straining work amongst the playful, amusing, mathematically-challenging, outrageous, levitational and hilarious. My suggestion would be to dip into it over the course of weeks or months, always seeking whatever suits your present mood or mind-state as *All That Is Evident* is a panorama, a cornucopia. As Monk concludes his pithy introduction – *Bon voyage!*

Personal Connection

My introduction to the Oulipo began in 1989 upon finding out a performer in the HAMLET I was directing was not only as interested in great literature as myself but much better informed. He spoke about the Oulipo in vague terms and told me to start by reading *Life*. Being poor I could not just go out and buy it but I certainly put it on the Book List that accompanied me on every visit to Toronto's then-multitude of used-book stores. It took over five years before, in disbelief, I finally chanced upon it, innocently reposing on its side atop a neat book-row, calmly awaiting my rapacious lunge. I started reading *Life* that night and before long arrived at its final pages.

Around that time John Delacourt became DNA's Dramaturge and being one of those people who seemingly does nothing else with his life other than read and write was of course familiar with the Oulipo and had hoovered *Life*. As my curiosity continued to be aroused, he told me the next step was to acquire the *Compendium*. Soon I was dipping into it whenever time and energy allowed – which was actually not that often seeing as DNA was all-consuming and my knowledge of literature had vast lacunae whimpering to be dispelled. Nevertheless, amidst forays into Balzac, Proust, Dostoyevsky, Stendhal, Javier Marias, among so many others, I slowly began to accumulate at least passable understanding of some Oulipian methodologies as I familiarized myself with examples of centos; univocalisms; x mistakes y for z; cylinders; irrational sonnets; avalanches; and snowballs (both expanding and melting). Curiosity blossomed into fascination.

In a way my intrigue with the Oulipo made perfect sense: I had always considered DNA's work to be "radical" and here was a group also dedicated to creations via "radical" means. I find so interesting conceptually – and stimulating intellectually – the very idea of designing a complex of precise, rigorous restrictions before even beginning the concrete realization of a new poem or ballet. Perec and others have stated how liberating constraints may be – however working within them is not only distinctly challenging but will usually lead you in surprising directions producing unanticipated results. The cerebral cortex obliged to work in unaccustomed ways excites the artist in me and I have felt that excitement tremble into thrill when in the midst of composition.

Upon reflection it was a little stunning to realize, only recently, I myself had created quasi-Oulipian, even unassailably Oulipian work – without ever being aware of it. The DNA *corpus* contains such disparate exultations it is dangerous to generalize but as the formation-process has often consisted of piling up an onerous succession of rules – some before rehearsal, some during – no wonder the finished work had a unique, "radical," even occasionally Oulipian, feel to it.

Technically speaking I cannot be considered an "anticipatory plagiarist" as my first work dates from 1982, over 20 years after the Oulipo was founded. As a case in point, however, the structure of that piece, POUND FOR POUND, followed the strictures of the ancient musical *crab* (or retrograde) *canon* wherein the accompaniment line is the melodic one's reverse – *my beginning is my end and my end is my beginning*. I liken the effect of that work to unrolling a carpet before rolling it up again. In DNA's case the musical lines were instead a polyphony of Pound poems. If you think once the half-way mark is reached the piece "automatically" writes itself you would be mistaken. The composer was always allowed – for variation, aesthetic pleasure, sheer bedevilment – alterations from the original: call them clinamens if you will. I find all this most curious. That centuries-old *canon cancrizans* seems a most Oulipian work; it seems equally obvious my creative DNA contained quite a few Oulipian genes; while composing that Pound-piece I certainly was ignorant of the Oulipo's existence. So if not an "anticipatory plagiarist" was I a "benighted plagiarist"?

One indisputably Oulipian DNA work was the FATE ballet of 2004, a time I *was* keenly aware of all those rats in their tortuous labyrinths. I say "indisputably" because the complete rules-assembly – restrictions, constraints, rules, they all amount to the same thing – was not only put in place before the first one-on-one encounter with the first dancer but adhered to throughout the 16-month rehearsal process. Yet these rules were all cobbled together, after much reflection, purely in choreographic service to the ballet, not because of my desire to fashion one in adherence to Oulipian principles. Once a "benighted plagiarist" always a "benighted plagiarist"?

Whatever category – if any – I belong to, it seems clear that beyond other abnormal or subversive strategies employed, constraints-use is a key part of what has made DNA work "radical" and so different from other theatre productions. Oulipian techniques have become ever-present tools at my disposal. They offer exciting, challenging possibilities. They present new ways of devising attack-modes and new routes for getting out of jams. It is indisputable: Oulipo-awareness allows me fresh approaches and sensibilities for making art.

THE CHALLENGE

Birth of the Challenge

Roughly one-third into *A Void*, the sleuths discover five famous poems and the grandest soliloquy of all, Hamlet's "To be or not to be," all E-deprived. I found Adair's rendering weak, unprobing, disappointing. Enter *hubris* – I thought I could produce a better version and soon began, proceeding in a leisurely manner. After about a month I invited two very intelligent and highly literate friends to join me: DNA's then-Board-President Gregory Nixon and Dramaturge John Delacourt. The idea was each of us would work in solitude and share our results at the challenge-dinner.

I outlined our task – to recreate "To be or not to be," starting with the first words and ending with "And lose the name of action." – followed by the restrictions:

1 no E's

2 you must express Shakespeare's words / meaning in your own way

3 your version must be grammatically correct, just like Shakespeare's

4 you cannot use an apostrophe to indicate a missing E (for example – lov'd, forgott'n)

5 foreign words are allowed *only* if they are in common English usage (for example – croissant, faux pas)

6 you do not have to obey Shakespeare's punctuation or capital letters or line-arrangements

* * *

Soon after starting, Gregory and I invited over the sprightly Paul Halferty, then in throes of completing his Ph.D. thesis, now working its way into the first history of Toronto's gay theatre. In the midst of telling us about the plays he would be imparting his wisdom on at his first full-time teaching job in Dublin, Paul excused himself from summer-evening's soothing glow to go for a pee. I leaned in to Gregory – *What do you think about asking Paul to be the Judge? He wouldn't have to provide a version himself, just listen to ours and be an impartial adjudicator.* Gregory was immediately in favour – *I think that's a great idea.*

When Paul re-joined us, I put the question to him straightaway. He demurred – poetry did not lie in his field of expertise. I jumped – *What are you talking about? It's not a* poem, *it's a soliloquy. It's part of a play. You're going to tell me plays don't lie in your so-called field of expertise? You're just about to begin teaching a university course on them.* As most anyone in today's Western "civilization," Paul feels continually pressed for time, wary of taking on yet another obligation. Again I sprang up – *Paul, for God's sake, it's only an evening,* one evening. *It'll be fun. And besides, you'll get to eat and drink well.* He then expressed some vague sense of insecurity, not being qualified, feeling incapable of doing a good job. I was beginning to lose any vestige of patience – *Right. You're starting to insult me. You think I'm inviting some idiot to preside over our mighty labours? You think you can't match wits with us three? For whatever good, we've all got university degrees between us. But who's on the verge of becoming a Doctor, for fuck's sake?* I then softened – *Look, Paul, we really want you to do this. We think you'd be the perfect person.*

It took half an hour for him to finally succumb. Was he badgered, browbeaten? Yes. Might he finally have been beguiled? That is the question. We'll never know.

* * *

Once a Judge had been anointed I began compiling criteria for judgment as well as formulating the agenda on which I imposed a degree of severity and precision, believing a degree of formality to be in line with Oulipian practices. Soon all participants were mailed the official protocol.

The Oulipo Challenge
Sat Oct 13, 2012, 4 pm – Procedural Rules

I have divided the soliloquy into 6 chunks, as follows, in order, starting w/ the following words:

7 to be or not to be:

8 to die: to sleep;

9 to die: to sleep;

10 for who would bear ...

11 who would fardels bear,

12 thus conscience does make ...

(a reminder that the soliloquy's last words, for our purposes, are "and lose the name of action")

* * *

1 upon arrival, each challenger must present the Judge with his final version (divided into the six chunks) which must not be altered after that presentation – thus the Judge must arrive shortly before 4 pm

2 everyone will take part in the Oulipo-cocktail preparation + dinner prep

3 the Judge will prepare lots to be drawn by the challengers in order to determine the order of presentation which will be maintained throughout

4 Hillar will read a brief quote by the physicist Hermann Weyl

5 the Judge will read the first chunk of Shakespeare's soliloquy

6 the first challenger (in the order determined by the draw) will read his version of the chunk followed by the other two challengers

7 the challengers will discuss each others' versions – the Judge will not partake in any discussion, will maintain his silence, but will listen attentively as challengers' comments might sway his scoring

8 when that discussion is finished – or when the Judge calls a stop to it – then

9 silence will ensue as the Judge records his scores for that chunk and adds any notes for future reference

* * *

Scoring

one point – for accuracy in the conveyance of Shakespeare's meaning

one point – grammatical correctness

up to three points – for originality / ingenuity / brilliance / beauty / poeticism

every letter E in a challenger's version will result in the deduction of one point

thus the maximum points to be awarded any challenger (per chunk) is five and since there are six chunks, the perfect score attainable is thirty

* * *

10   the Judge will read the next chunk of the soliloquy followed by the challengers' versions – I hope it is clear that if the draw determines the order to be Gregory, Hillar, John, then the second round would be Hillar, John, Gregory, etc. – thus each challenger will go first and last thrice – followed by the discussion amongst challengers, the Judge's scoring and then on to the next chunk

11 when all the versions have been presented, Hillar, with due probity and circumspection, will announce a revelation

12 the Judge will present the revelation follow-up

13 the Judge will announce the scores for the first chunk along with his comments, justification, praise, condemnation – challengers' response might well ensue – and then the Judge will announce the next chunk's scores, etc., until he reaches the end and the winner becomes apparent

14 dinner, not a collation, with fine wines

The Challenge
4 pm – Preamble

Everyone arrived on time and handed the six soliloquy-chunks to Judge Halferty, each chunk on a separate sheet of paper. Delacourt stunned us with news he had got married the previous month. Congratulations all round.

Everyone then busied themselves with either preparing the lamb for roasting or making the "Oulipo cocktail," first created to make more pleasurable that aforementioned "seminar" I conducted for two friends.

For those wishing to add a touch of authenticity while reading the transcript – not a bad idea – follow these instructions:

1 juice 2-dozen ripe mandarins and if wishing a sour-dart add two (ideally pink) grapefruits into the mix

2 pulp 3 ripe mangoes, ideally the flat oblong yellow-skinned ones (called the Ataúlfo)

3 blend juice and pulp until very well integrated

4 pour into tall glass the desired measure of ice-cold vodka and add a healthy dose of the juice-pulp blend, leaving enough room to add a little organic lemonade

5 as the juice-pulp blend will be of thickish consistency, the vodka will rise to the top and you must stir glass-contents with vigour before your first sip

* * *

We drew lots to establish order of contestants' readings; with each chunk the Judge would read Shakespeare's original and then distribute the contestants their versions; these would be returned to the Judge when all were ready to move on to the next chunk.

Preparations completed, roast in oven, glasses in hand, procedure established, we seated ourselves at kitchen's large wooden table, the Judge appropriately at its head. A high-quality omni-directional digital recorder was placed in table's centre.

Notes to the Transcript

This transcript has been edited as faithfully as possible, a far from easy task.

One must understand what transpired was a serious conversation among four people who much liked and respected each other. On the other hand, the occasion had celebration's feel: all three contestants excitable, drinking, continually interrupting and talking over each other. The Judge, most fittingly, displayed cool-headed sobriety throughout.

People often spoke in phrases, heedless of correct grammar and an accurate transcription would be helplessly infested with colloquialisms, conversation-fillers ("um", "ah", "you know" being a Delacourt specialty), repetition-laden think-alouds (a Hillar affliction), correct-word searchings and incomplete sentences. Some of the above have been retained to impart occasion's flavour whereas others (meandering digressions, tediously clarified miscomprehensions) considered unhelpful and bogging down the reader have not been included. On occasion a few words have been added, in square brackets, in order to admit clarity.

Were all chuckles, snorts and laughter-explosions here noted the result would be an intolerable document. A particularly glaring example would be Delacourt almost inevitably responding to Hillar and Gregory's chunk-readings with a resounding "Ohhohohohoho!" His admixtures of surprise, admiration and amusement – along with other such non-essentials – have mostly been deleted.

A few quotes are necessarily omitted due to insufficient volume on the speaker's part or voices hopelessly buried under continual paper-shufflings, chair-movings and the like.

Myself, as transcriber, recognize the inevitable prejudices inherent in deciding upon condensations and elisions, insist I have done my best to be accurate and hope the resultant transcript conveys the essence of an event most memorable, tinged with heartfelt but competitive camaraderie, occasional prickle-smatters and fuelled by underlying tensely-coiled energy which occasionally erupted with striking urgency.

Dramatis Personae

PH – Paul Halferty – Judge

JD – John Delacourt
HL – Hillar Liitoja
GN – Gregory Nixon

The Challenge
4:45 pm

PH: So Hillar, I believe you will read a quote.

HL: I will.

PH: From Hermann Weyl?

HL: I don't know how you pronounce his name, I just know he's a physicist. And the quote is as follows – *I always try to combine the true with the beautiful, but when I have to choose one or the other, I usually choose the beautiful.* Isn't that lovely? From a *physicist*? You always think beauty, but ultimately …

JD: Yeah.

PH: OK, So the Judge will read the first chunk of the Shakespeare soliloquy.

> **To be, or not to be: that is the question:**
> **Whether 'tis nobler in the mind to suffer**
> **The slings and arrows of outrageous fortune,**
> **Or to take arms against a sea of troubles,**
> **And by opposing end them?**

JD: So now I read my version?

HL: Yes.

JD: This daily dying or this nightly living; which prevails?
   What if nobility lay in withstanding, all mind manacling
   Wounds a man will sustain from want of luck's dark turns?
   Or if it lay in arming his soul to fight such wild swings
   of luck, night-born,
   And brought to ground?

HL: Let's get that all over again, please.

PH: Yeah.

HL: That was just ... huge.

[John rereads the chunk.]

GN: Do I just go ahead now?

HL: Unless anybody wants to comment. I thought that was pretty fucking awesome.

PH: I might ask for them to be read again.

GN: You should just cue us, let each of us know when it's time to go.

PH: Gregory.

GN: To act or not to act, this is our quandary
   Is our moral high-ground found by stoically rolling with
   myriad blows,
   That fortuitous position will attract,
   Or is it found through action, by mounting an attack,
   On a vast array of all that assails,
   And by doing so, bring that array to naught.

JD: Ohhohohohoho!

HL: Again please.

[Gregory rereads the chunk.]

PH: Hillar.

HL: To stay on living or not: that is what confounds us.
Which would satisfy honour's most fair claim –
To sustain both slings and arrows of lunatic luck –
or to summon arms against a whirl of hardship
and by opposing, vanquish all?

JD: Well played, gentlemen.

[Uproarious laughter provoked by undue formality.]

GN: Let's hear it a second time.

[Hillar rereads the chunk.]

GN: Mighty fine.

HL: You know, what strikes me is how different the three of us are, meaning the three versions are. Yet, I think I would say each one of us got the essence of it and ...

JD: It would be really interesting to hear somebody who doesn't know what we're working from, what they are picking up too ... if you told them this was based on something ... because there are resonances still of the actual soliloquy that you can get, a lot of resonances.

HL: I'm not sure exactly what your point is. You were saying if there was somebody who was sitting over there who had no idea why we had convened ...

JD: No, who knew *why* we had convened but did not know *the soliloquy* we were basing this on.

HL: I don't think it would take long for them to figure it out.

JD: Well, it depends how old they are. You know they don't get Shakespeare [in school] anymore, right? So …

HL: I loved your "mind manacling." Where was the context of that?

JD: "'tis nobler in the mind to suffer" … all "mind manacling wounds" rather than "slings and arrows."

GN: That was really nice, John.

HL: I just think that was gorgeous.

GN: So what happens now? Do you need to take some time?

PH: This is a very difficult task …

GN: It is.

PH: … that is set before me. I would like to actually look at them. You can continue speaking if you like. We might want to hear them again, too. I'm just going to have a look at them.

JD: Sure.

HL: We've been slaving away and now the Judge is going – *This is SO hard.*

JD: It *was* fucking hard though. I don't know about you, but …

GN: Hard – but inspiring at the same time too. I found it really interesting the kinds of discoveries that you make.

JD: Me too.

GN: Certainly the first direction I went was not the one I ended up sticking with.

JD: It would be great to do a soliloquy like this … imagine doing it at different points in your life too, how much your own experience weighs into your "translation." That's what I thought interesting. Because I haven't approached this soliloquy for at least a decade, I haven't looked at it. Recently, before doing this, I put *Hamlet* on my iPad just to go back to it, but this was my first pass with *Hamlet* in about ten years.

HL: For me it's been since 1989, that's when I did my HAMLET so I have not … I fucking *slaved* over it.

JD: For you it is now in your bloodstream.

HL: Well it's strange because I could not … I could whip off the first lines from memory and that's it. And what was so interesting is just I know my interpretation of what it means, what is Shakespeare saying, changed from 1989 to …

GN: Mine totally did [during] this exercise, my interpretation of it changed …

JD: That's what I mean, completely.

GN: And not only that but also I noticed there was at least one little section in it that I wasn't entirely clear in its meaning. And every time I'd read the thing before I just kind of glossed right through it – that's totally fine, it's not that important, but now that I'm going through it word by word I'm going – *I'd never actually sat down and tried to figure out what this means.*

JD: I found it in the syntax as much as I found it in the words. All of a sudden, OK, *this* is how it comes together.

HL: I wonder if it's the exact same spot as me because when this [challenge] was just between Gregory and me what happened was John came over and I asked him a few questions – *What the fuck does this mean anyway?* And we talked through …

GN: I feel better now.

HL: We basically talked it through and, by the way, I still have those notes … and it wasn't like John was going – *OK, Hillar, this means this, this means that.* Sure, there were a couple of obvious ones but there were a couple of other ones that were …

JD: Yeah, where it was like – *Wait a second here …*

GN: We should talk about those when it's all over, which were the spots cause it's quite interesting. But don't you also feel like you know the text better now than …

JD: Oh, for sure.

HL: Yes.

GN: What an incredible way of digging deep into text. It should be like … English classes should do this or theatre classes should say: "OK, pick a soliloquy and …"

JD: And we're going to give you constraints and push for meaning here …

HL: (*to the Judge*) When you actually have decided on the marks, you're going to make sure we don't see you …

PH: I'll discuss the marks later.

HL: No, my point is this. I'm assuming, correct me if I'm wrong, but when you're done with your study of the first chunk, you are going to mark it on the chart but make sure that we don't see it …

PH: OK

HL: … and then hide it, so when we start chunk two there'll be a blank, you know what I mean?

PH: Yes.

JD: Jonathan Miller, the director, he talks about when he actually tries to interpret Shakespeare it's like a Necker cube where …

HL: Like a *what*?

JD: A Necker cube. Now this is something that I guess they discovered over the last two hundred years. It's a little bit of perception theory as well. There's that drawing that Wittgenstein showed people. You can see it as a woman or you could see it as a man with a beard.

GN: But you couldn't see the same thing, I mean both at the same time.

JD: Exactly. There was this curious kind of pivoting in terms of your perceptions. I was thinking through what Miller said – *That's what Shakespeare does. It pivots and it can go this way or that way and you can go either way with it.*

PH: I have a question about the criteria for each of you. What does "accuracy" mean?

GN: That's tricky because the way I interpreted accuracy was basically *meaning* … as long as you maintained the meaning. So if there's a key sentence, it's not left out of your thing, as long as you got the elements in there in a way that can be understood. That would be my interpretation.

HL: I agree totally with Gregory. I would put it a slightly different way. And that is, number one, you have to decide what exactly is Shakespeare saying here. And then you put it into your own words, into words that are non-E.

PH: So that would be also similar to Gregory.

HL: Very, very similar. It's essentially the same thing.

JD: Same with me. A lot of what you're dealing with here are abstractions, of course, but it's like – Is there an equivalence with subject? Is there an equivalence with verb? Is there an equivalence with object? And is it ballpark, even when we're dealing with abstractions? Does it at least follow that the verb is working to connect this up?

GN: And is it all there? If he's got something in there, you didn't just gloss over it, it's there in yours as well.

HL: And you didn't have flights of fancy where you're making your own interpretation completely, [imagining] what he's really *meaning* to say is …

PH: Right.

GN: So what do we do? Should we leave the room for a couple of minutes while …

[*The Judge collects his thoughts.*]

PH: And so for "grammatical correctness," I'll ask the same question – what does it mean for you?

HL: Well, the soliloquy is grammatically correct and so our thing should also be grammatically correct. Poetic, yes, if we want, yes, we can stretch that, but essentially it should follow the basic rules of grammar, the basic rules of syntax.

JD: Exactly.

GN: Some things you do really have to change significantly …

JD: Exactly.

GN: … but you still have to be grammatically correct.

JD: You gotta bring it back.

HL: Exactly. You've got to bring it back. Beautifully put. Cause that's what I found also … is that you'd have to go out on a limb but then you'd pull yourself back. You can't just take each line and put it into non-E words and then end up with something that's not grammatically correct.

JD: That's what I found a real challenge here because so much of the verb structure relies on that E.

PH: And now, there are no E's. I don't think any of you used E's in this one. So there are no deductions to be made.

GN: Good. I know I went through mine a dozen times, there are no E's in mine, I can pretty much guarantee … unless I misspelled something.

JD: I was so close too …

GN: Oh, but I caught myself a couple of times, I found the occasional "the" popping up and I was like – *Whoa, glad I caught that.*

JD: Me too.

HL: Magda saved me. [*Magda Vasko is DNA's Associate Artist.*]

JD: Did she?

GN: You had an editor. You had a copy editor, my God!

JD: Wow!

HL: She caught an E.

JD: Next time I'm calling Magda, that's it then, level the playing field.

HL: I had an enormous difficulty with that. I don't know why but I had *enormous* difficulty. I would read it …

JD: … and not see it.

HL: You know what my first version was? It started off "To keep living on or not". And I lived with that for *weeks*. And then I went – *Wait! These are E's, Hillar.*

JD: I thought "eel" this morning and I thought – *What the fuck?* I know exactly …

HL: [They're just so] sneaky, you're so used to them that you're …

GN: You read right over them. You don't even *see* them.

JD: That is a fine cocktail.

GN: Isn't it lovely?

PH: This is very difficult.

HL: And you know you are *not* announcing results yet.

PH: No, I'm just …

HL: Bitching.

PH: … expressing the difficulty.

GN: I can imagine it's probably difficult.

[*The Judge clarifies the scoring once more as he begins to decide our chunk-scores. No half-points.*]

HL: Every E is a minus one. So if I would have written "To keep on living …" I would have been down two points right off the start. Out goes the accuracy!

GN: Oh yeah, it's a point *per* E.

PH: (to John) You have an E.

JD: Oh no!

HL: No!

JD: Where is it?

PH: "which *prevails.*"

JD: Oh my God!

HL: They're *brutal.*

JD: Thank God you caught it.

PH: I'd better just look for E's at this moment.

JD: It's so …

GN: We were just talking about it …

JD: Exactly.

PH: I did not notice either.

JD: I just love the rhythm. What can I tell you? It's an iamb.

HL: At least "iamb" doesn't have an E in it …

JD: Exactly.

HL: I'm repeating myself but it's *outrageous* how those E's became invisible. They're just …

JD: I know.

HL: Just like with "prevail." I didn't catch it, he read it *twice.*

GN: I'm surprised I didn't catch it cause it's a word I thought of a couple of times.

HL: Did this also happen to you? That you're looking for an appropriate word? So it's got an E in it, out. What about *this* word? Oh, it's also got an E. What about *this* word? Oh, it's *also* got an E.

GN: You know why I think that is? I was thinking about that very thing a lot during this and I think it's because related words often have the same letters in them.

JD: Yes, yes.

GN: Like for example you'd be looking for a word – *Oh, I can't use the word "result"* – so then you're like OK, and then every word you come up with has an E … "resolution" …or "verdict" … or whatever. And it's the same kind of spot because they're related to each other.

HL: And wasn't that infuriating?

JD: Yes.

HL: You're at your fifth word and you just go – *OK, I just have to work around this, I've got to …*

JD: Yeah.

HL: … *reconfigure it differently.*

PH: I'm going to ask that each of you read it one last time and I've made what we'll call "interim marks" and I just want to hear them one last time and decide I am indeed happy with the marks I have assigned. So we'll begin with you, John.

[*All three of us reread the first chunk.*]

PH: OK, I, with some trepidation, make my …

GN: It's a tough gig, man.

PH: It's a very tough gig … very tough.

HL: At least you're not being grilled, OK?

PH: Oh, I anticipate that I might be by the end.

HL: No, I mean it's going to be the *lamb* that gets roasted.

PH: Right. Shall we stop?

JD: Sure.

[*Everyone but the Judge goes on the porch for a cigarette break. Upon return …*]

PH: I shall read.

> To die: to sleep;
> No more; and by a sleep to say we end
> The heart-ache and the thousand natural shocks
> That flesh is heir to, 'tis a consummation
> Devoutly to be wish'd.

Gregory.

GN: Oh that I could avoid choosing and simply go rightly numb.
> To blunt my waking condition at last
> And spirit mind and body away from pain's many jolts and jabs,
> Paroxysms born with my body.
> A void, oblivion, a thing I fondly wish for.

HL: Aaah! Nice. I'd love to hear that again.

JD: Me too.

[*Gregory rereads the chunk.*]

PH: Very good. Thank you. Hillar.

HL: To attain your infinity-long black-out –
> that's all. And by that finality to stop
> all soul-pangs, all manifold natural shocks
> that physicality inflicts upon us, 'tis a consummation
> to avidly long for.

JD: Can we get that one more time?

PH: Yes, please. Hillar.

[*Hillar rereads the chunk.*]

PH: Thank you. John.

JD: **A daily dying; adrift on wormwood thoughts**
All for nought; such drifting cast as final,
No hurt remaining, all such wounds
A body will withstand to mark a sum
This is a wish to tally.

HL: Remaining? *RE*maining? Spelled the Estonian way, R, O with a snake over it …?

JD: I actually meant "no hurt Romanians". [*Explosive laughter due to claim's preposterous nature.*] There is a whole part of *Hamlet* where the Romanians …

GN: The melancholy Romanians …

PH: May I have it again?

HL: Wormwood.

JD: Afterwards I'll explain why I love this word.

[*John rereads the chunk.*]

JD: When you are tallying up that part, it *is* that Estonian spelling of 'remaining' that I …

PH: The other thing that I realize now when I hear the second bit is I should actually look at them as complete wholes.

GN: You should.

JD: Yes.

GN: You should probably at the end read all of them all the way through.

PH: Yes, because I'm hearing now the themes or words that are reoccurring and how they're being expressed.

GN: I think this is an interesting discovery. We should probably leave you alone for fifteen minutes so you can read all three of them from beginning to end.

PH: Cause they *are* wholes.

HL: Or you can have each of us read from beginning to end but I think it would be impossible to digest, at least or me.

PH: But it may have an impact …

GN: Do you need us or is it now a good time to run out and have a cigarette?

PH: You can go have a cigarette.

JD: So *The Clock* is here … [*Christian Marclay's 24-hour film*] … until November twenty-something.

GN: It's here for another month, I think.

PH: I have to go, I haven't gone yet.

GN: You must.

[*The contestants retire to the porch for a cigarette. The recording is not turned off and we hear the Judge musing softly to himself about accuracy and … Upon return …*]

HL: So during our nicotine-break John explained wormwood. He got it from Revelations, where angels blow trumpets and then make pronouncements, all very awful to mankind and, in fact, all forms of life.

JD: After the third trumpet-call a great blazing star fell on many rivers, lakes and fresh-water sources making them very bitter. And that star was called Wormwood …

HL: … because the herb was known as being not only bitter but super-poisonous, deadly.

GN: So drinking any water was a gamble. Because this contaminated water could kill you.

JD: Exactly.

PH: So when you have Hamlet thinking of wormwood, he is contemplating it as a way of suicide.

JD: Yes.

PH: Thank you for clearing that up.

GN: Wormwood as hemlock, which killed Socrates, except it has an E.

JD: Yeah, hemlock would have been easier. But there's something interesting here. Chernobyl is the Ukrainian name for mugwort and mugwort is a species of artemesia. Artemesia is known as "common" wormwood. So when the nuclear meltdown happened, many Russians thought the end of the world was coming.

HL: So Chernobyl had Biblical connotations as well as everything else. Which reminds me. When Gregory was in Mexico some seven or eight weeks ago he was saying – *You know what? I could have a glass of real absinthe, not this fake absinthe but this real absinthe that's made of wormwood. But dammit, it costs fourteen dollars for just one shot and the bottle was $170.*

GN: It was 250 bucks for a bottle. But I was tempted.

HL: You guys are welcome to take up a collection ...

GN: For the next person who's going to Mexico.

HL: For the next person who's going to Mexico. [*that was Hillar's plan.*]

PH: Now I have a question cause thus far everyone's been quite ... not entirely silent but no one has said "that was really wonderful *but* ..." I wonder if you have any criticism for one another, I'll just throw that out there. We can pay attention to it in the next round. Or not. You don't have to.

JD: It *is* interesting. It's a good point because so much of this is, for me, performative. I'm listening to it almost like a performance and I'm not thinking critically, that's true.

HL: You know, it's strange, me also, because for example I think that your first line or two of the first chunk was not spot-on, but I would really have to study it, I would have to sit down ... but just on first or second hearing I was dubious – but I would say "oh, come on" if you were ...

PH: ... if you were way off.

JD: Yeah.

GN: I haven't heard anything like that.

JD: Yeah.

GN: I think there's an interesting discussion to be had about approaches and broader choices but I wouldn't want to have that discussion until we've gone through it all.

PH: I think my experience of what's happening right now seems quite different from your experience of what's happening right now. Which is fine.

HL: Well, you've got a different role to play. For us it's kind of like "Job Done"! And this is the fun part.

JD: For sure. Part of it too is that with such constraints, for me, it is interesting to see the amount of play, "play" meaning the variations ...

HL: That was evident from the first one.

JD: Yeah, and what you're seeing is something like how a mind works, which is kind of fascinating, how a compositional intelligence is working from piece to piece. And so, again, I'm not suggesting I've totally taken critical faculties and put them aside.

HL: Me neither. And I'm really glad we've got a Judge ...

GN + JD: Me too.

HL: ... who was out of the process and can look at it from a really dispassionate point of view. Because I feel very strongly about what I have done.

JD: Me too. It's almost like what I want to do is say – *Let me tell you how I wrestled with* ... but that's for later.

PH: OK, so now, Hillar, I believe you are first.

HL: I would like another drink.

GN: Vodka's almost gone.

HL: I'm going to get another bottle of vodka.

[*Drinks are served.*]

PH: To die, to sleep;
   To sleep: perhaps to dream: ay, there's the rub;
   For in that sleep of death what dreams may come
   When we have shuffled off this mortal coil,
   Must give us pause: there's the respect
   That makes calamity of so long life;

GN: You were inaccurate on one word. It's "perchance" to dream. You said "perhaps".

PH: Excuse me. "perchance." Yes, that's how it's written.

GN: Want to give it another go?

PH: Sure. Yeah, that wasn't very well read, was it?

HL: No! [*much laughter at Hillar's vehemence.*] Now that you've opened up this criticism thing ...

[*The Judge rereads the chunk correctly and with more feeling.*]

PH: How was that? Better?

GN: Much.

PH: [to *Hillar*] I shall be extra critical on you next time.

HL: You're welcome to be as critical as you like. In fact, that makes me think of that lovely title of ... who's that art critic?

GN: Robert Hughes?

JD: *Nothing if not Critical.*

HL: Glorious title.

PH: OK. Hillar.

HL: To mortuary, to black-out –
      to black-out: who knows, to host subconscious visions:
      what a quandary!
      For in that dormancy of black infinity what visions may
      us haunt
      as cast off is this mortal coil,
      must halt our thoughts. This abiding doubt
      marks with calamity so long a visitation in our world.

JD: Once more?

[*Hillar rereads chunk 3.*]

PH: Thank you. So you're next, John.

JD: A night-living; adrift on wormwood thoughts
      Or such thoughts on wing, took flight from logic's
      grasp; sadly
      All ills of soul-sick living form from such flight
      And at last burn out within a body, not a mark on it but
      an Icarus scar,
      Though such a firm FINIS should ground our thoughts
      – for thusly
      All days add up to nought but calamity.

HL: Fuck me! Icarus scars? Aah!

[*John rereads chunk 3.*]

HL: Nice. And we've got the first use so far of a foreign word, that is …

JD: Finis.

HL: I think … I would certainly allow it, it's certainly part of the …

GN: That's part of the English vernacular.

JD: It's fine. I think I'd be OK in Scrabble with it.

PH: Gregory.

GN: But what of oblivion if in word only it stays,
   A canvas not blank but full with somnambulistic illusions,
   And additional acts of our plays.
   What a bitch that is. For in a void what visions will
   visitations pay,
   What traumas still to unfold,
   As our corpora grind down to ash and clay.
   Our minds hold onto this thought and in this way,
   Our instinct to hang on through thick and thin holds
   us so taut,
   That quixotic fancy cannot signal us astray.

HL: I got little chills there. Fuck me! Wow!

GN: Thanks.

JD: That was gorgeous. Sorry, we're criticizing now I realize. As soon as you bring that into the room it hangs there.

PH: That's fine.

HL: There's something very special about that.

PH: Once more.

[Gregory rereads chunk 3.]

HL: I've got a problem. Corpora?

GN: Corpora.

HL: Latin?

GN: No, English. It's the plural of corpus.

JD: Wow!

HL: Corpus, corpora.

GN: Corpora is the plural of corpus. In English. I looked it up.

HL: Really? OK.

GN: It's literally from the Latin but …

HL: Because the Latin plural would be corporae, which would have an E. And yours is plural, so …

GN: I looked it up. Corpus is the singular, corpora is the plural.

JD: Wow.

HL: Nice.

JD: Yeah, beautiful – corpora ground to ash and clay.

HL: Particularly gorgeous when you think of "from dust to dust". What is it?

PH: "Ashes to ashes, dust to dust."

HL: And that's *so* lovely to have …

JD: And it's the first one actually where the register shifts, where we go into a complete sort of idiomatic … "what a bitch."

HL: I loved your quixotic and I loved canvas …

JD: Yeah.

HL: … cause there is this sense of … it's blank and big, not that a canvas has to be blank and big, but when you say canvas, what I conjure right away is this …

JD: Expanse.

HL: … expanse and limitless possibilities.

GN: It's glorious hearing all this great stuff you guys have done.

JD: So much of it is translation too … cause I think we've wrestled with the text so much.

HL: Corpus, corpora, quixotic, canvas, I'm just really taken by what you did and I just feel like I'm repeating myself but I'm *astonished* at the wide range.

GN: It's very interesting.

JD: Yeah.

HL: What I *love* is that everybody is recasting it.

JD: Yeah.

HL: We're not going word by word by word, we're basically saying – *What's going on here? What is the essence of what he's trying to say and how am I now going to* …

JD: Embody it.

HL: … *in E-less words?* And it's kind of what you said out there [on the porch], it's like a staggering beauty can come out of this restriction, because you would think the restriction …

JD: … would limit the range.

HL: … boots out all kinds of things, whereas …

GN: That's the whole idea of the Oulipo …

JD: Exactly.

GN: … that you discover new worlds by your restrictions.

JD: Yeah.

GN: I have a question about the last round and it's probably something I completely missed. But I think there's great significance in that line "ay, there's the rub."

JD: Yeah, because there is a turn …

GN: I did "what a bitch that is" and Hillar, you definitely did have it, but John, did you have it in yours?

JD: Let me go back …

GN: I was listening for it and I didn't … cause he's basically saying "here's the nut of it all" and I think that statement …

PH: "ay, there's the rub," where is that?

JD: What I've got is "sadly all ills of soul-sick living form from such flight." You're not getting it because I don't think the register shifts.

GN: Right. OK. It's the one place where Hamlet kind of goes – *Listen, I'm discovering the nut, I'm pulling it open.* I went quite far with it, "What a bitch that is."

JD: And it grounded beautifully because you shifted the register – which I thought really worked. All of a sudden it becomes "voom," you get it right to the fore.

HL: I didn't go quite as far as you did, my "what a quandary!" is the same kind of colloquialism almost. Can we have John's for a moment. Cause I didn't understand where you were.

JD: "To sleep: perchance to dream: ay, there's the rub; for in that sleep of death what dreams may come." And mine wraps around this phrase "adrift on wormwood thoughts or such thoughts on wing, took flight from logic's grasp; sadly all ills of soul-sick living."

HL: So "ay, there's the rub" is just basically for you "sadly."

JD: Yes. Essentially I wrap the meaning around "ay, there's the rub" into all of this here.

HL: Something I think everybody does that I also found really interesting. So just because Shakespeare says "to die" [a couple of times] doesn't necessarily mean if you find the solution to "to die" that you've got to repeat your solution.

JD: Absolutely.

HL: The first time I went through it, I was more mechanical and then I went – *Wait a minute, no.*

JD: You can turn it. Exactly.

HL: Yours might have been even better if you'd said "What a bitch." as opposed to "What a bitch that is."

JD: It's just … the pause just works really well.

GN: Yeah, but I needed the extra syllables to make it …

HL: There's the *other* thing. I found myself adding …

GN: Or cutting. I actually cut a couple of things …

HL: … cut or add, just to get the rhythm, the poetic flow.

JD: The music.

HL: The music, yeah. So for me, for example, in this case I didn't go "To die, to sleep" … basically he means the same thing so that's why I just went "infinity-long blackout" as opposed to trying to decode "to die" and then "to sleep."

JD: "perchance to dream."

HL: By the way, I really struggled between two words there, I'd love your take on it. I think my take on "to dream" had to do with "subconscious vision."

JD: Yeah.

HL: Do you think "unconscious" would have been better? You see, the beauty of "unconscious" is that when you're dead you're not awake. But on the other hand the "subconscious vision" means your soul is there.

JD: I think "subconscious" because I go back to actually what's going on with *him* throughout, I can't help but see …

HL: Hamlet?

JD: Yeah. Because through so much of it he's hearing his dad all the time.

HL: I never thought about Hamlet at *all*. I didn't think about Hamlet *once*, what he was going through when saying this. I didn't for a moment put myself … *I* was Hamlet. *I* was the one who …

JD: Yeah.

HL: Hamlet never even occurred to me. [*Gregory laughs.*] And you're saying the same thing [as John]?

GN: Pretty much, yeah.

HL: So you were going "so what's going though Hamlet's mind?"

JD: No, actually, I wasn't either. Only what's happening in his *dreams*.

GN: I think "subconscious" is more appropriate because you're referring to the word "dream" and the dream is informed by the subconscious, not the unconscious.

HL: But he's dead.

GN: But what he's comparing is … he's talking about the dream. If we go to sleep and have dreams then when we die, is there an equivalent to that? And the closest we can get to imagining it would be the subconscious.

HL: Thank you.

JD: That's why I came up with this "a nightly living and a daily dying." That's what it relates to. The "nightly living" is the life that occurs in the dream.

GN: That's a really nice motif. You've used it twice now.

HL: Well, thanks for explaining that.

PH: You can be in a dream state but it's not a state in itself. Whereas unconscious is a state. You *are* unconscious. *Subconscious* is a kind of thing. Dreams are kinds of things that you *have* rather than things that you *are*.

HL: I think a different way of putting it is if you're unconscious you can't really dream.

PH: Well, dreams happen when you are unconscious apparently, right?

HL: When I sleep, am I unconscious?

PH: You are unconscious.

HL: I am, eh?

PH: Yes.

JD: Really?

HL: I thought I needed to be …

JD: … like knocked out cold?

HL: Like half a bottle of vodka.

JD: Me too.

PH: I don't know. Maybe I'm wrong.

GN: That's a semantic discussion around the word unconscious.

PH: I'm sure the dictionary would say ... Shall we move on the next?

GN: Sure.

HL: If you're ready for it.

GN: Any questions from the Judge?

PH: No, this is very difficult because ...

HL: Ooooh!

PH: Yeah, it's just a difficult thing.

HL: *Really*? [*sarcasm*]

PH: I say "difficult" again because things are unfolding and I'm making judgments on bits. And then I'm realizing that the bits go together and they go together for particular reasons. And it's also I have felt the urge to give bonus marks at particular moments, but I cannot do that.

HL: But in your comments you can certainly say – *Fuck, I could only give three to poetic because I would have liked to have given it five.*

PH: OK. Shall we begin?

HL: You're the Judge.

PH: Are you ready?

HL: Yeah, I think we're ready.

JD: I'm ready.

GN: Use your big stick, Judge, get us in line.

JD: Cause we will get out of it.

GN: Unruly pack of kids.

PH: OK. So chunk number 4.

> For who would bear the whips and scorns of time,
> The oppressor's wrong, the proud man's contumely,
> The pangs of despised love, the law's delay,
> The insolence of office and the spurns
> That patient merit of the unworthy takes,
> When he himself might his quietus make
> With a bare bodkin?

[Judge reads it a second time due to stumblings, mispronunciation and a skipped word. The third time was also problematic, prompting corrections.]

Shall we begin? Before the Judge gets bitchy?

JD: Am I first?

GN: You are.

PH: Yes.

HL: This is chunk 4. This is your last time to read first. Make the most if it!

JD: Alright.

> For who could sustain a kind of faith within that long
> spin of hours upon a clock,
> Withstand wounds unjust, words struck from casts to
> smash a proud man's will apart,
> Or such a parody of amor fati that is romantic fantasy,
> or a parodist's fantasy of a just world,
> Or a revolt of all that's plainly just … though in
> withstanding all
> A man may call this daily dying finally worth
> His sacrificial nightly living,
> With shiv in hand, why not?

HL: OK. You've got an E in there, baby.

JD: Whereabouts?

HL: Towards the end. Or middle.

JD: "revolt."

HL: Yeah.

JD: Oh, God! What the hell is going on? I'm going completely off the fucking reservation with this.

HL: Nicely put. Accurate assessment.

JD: Yes.

HL: Before you do it again, there's a word I want to ask you about. It sounded like "amphora."

JD: "amor fati."

GN: "amor fati"? What is that? Latin for crazy love? Unrequited love?

JD: No. Love that you are fated to.

HL: Is it two words?

JD: Two words, yes, "amor fati."

HL: You're really pushing the bounds of the English there. I mean I've never heard that expression before. "Amor," absolutely. "Fati" ... Have you heard people talk like that?

GN: It's new for me.

JD: The only reason I went there is I had it in my head first and then I went ... Regardless.

HL: OK.

[John rereads chunk 4.]

HL: "with shiv in hand, why not?" ... Nice. I really like that.

GN: Yeah, that's beautiful.

JD: It's almost like a catalogue of versions of what constitutes meaning.

HL: Also loved "a parodist's fantasy of a just world." Maybe this is a little premature but I found this the most difficult chunk.

JD: Although number five was difficult also.

PH: Gregory.

GN: For who would put up with such stabs and insults,
That mark our hourglass's sand caught fast in gravity's tug.
Bullying from landlord and boss, humiliations from
big-shot dicks,
Conjugal bliss withdrawn and lost, fair conclusions not
forthcoming,
Insults by official pricks.
Indulging fools unworthy as all of our clocks do tick,
Run through with a long knitting pin a fool would shut
up quick.

HL: Man, Gregory, man! Give us another 15 seconds and let's
hear it again.

JD: Blazing. Blazing.

HL: It's shocking how …

JD: And control.

[*Gregory rereads chunk 4.*]

HL: Nice.

JD: The "long knitting pin" as a weapon too … I love it.

HL: What's also delightful is if you're paying attention you
know what word he really wants to use and can't. And you can
see the gyrations.

PH: Hillar.

HL: For who would stand unstopping whips and scorns,
subjugator's wrongs, proud man's opprobrium,
all pangs of ardour's snubs, law's crawl
and haughty authority's looks – only to wallow,

with calm mind, in unworthy's spurns,
not choosing to succumb to his finality
by committing swift hara kiri?

GN: There are no E's in hara kiri?

HL: Only Is.

GN: Cause I thought of that word but I thought there was an E in there. Well done!

HL: Well done you too if you would have confirmed it. But your "long knitting pin" is also wonderful.

JD: One more time.

[*Hillar rereads chunk 4.*]

GN: Nice.

JD: Lovely.

HL: Thank you.

PH: Now it's interesting that you said ... Not to give my comments too early but essentially you said it was one of the most difficult ones because in many ways it was the clearest. Those were the clearest examples, like the relationship between the original text, for me. And your interpretation of that text was very clear.

GN: But so much of it is like a shopping list. It's like boom, boom, boom.

JD: You're just essentially translating a catalogue in your own way.

HL: Yeah.

GN: It was difficult to write, though, without E's. I found that one very difficult too.

HL: And in terms of meaning, what I had trouble with was "and the spurns that patient merit of the unworthy takes." Was that one ...

GN: That's the one ... Actually that whole section right there til the end I think ... "that patient merit" – indulging a fool, wasting your time on a fool – that's how I read that.

JD: Me too.

GN: And I think he's advocating violence, I think he's saying – *until the point when you just want to fucking run them through.*

JD: Yeah.

GN: Or let them do it to themselves. When it gets so bad you just want them dead, like you want the bare bodkin ...

JD: Yeah.

GN: ... his quietus make with bare bodkin ... or hara-kiri or whatever, when all you really want him to do is stab himself. That's how I read those last ...

HL: I read the "he himself" as relating to the beginning of the section "with who."

GN: I did too at first. But then I looked at it and I thought – *Because he says* "he himself" *I think he's deflecting it to the fool who's taking up his patience, who's taking his time.* I think this is him getting to his wits' end of the shopping list. Each one gets more ... He goes ... I'm not getting fucked, I'm not getting this, I'm not getting that and finally when you're spending so much time talking to a fucking idiot ... when he himself may quietus make ... shut up! ... by stabbing himself with a bare bodkin.

HL: I read it differently. I read it as – I'm going through this, this, this, this, this and I can escape it all by just going [*Hillar mimes shooting himself*].

PH: Yes.

GN: That's more consistent with the overall theme of the thing. I just thought … I like the idea that he's just getting to the point of – *Shut the fuck up! PLEASE!* He's at the end of his rope with it and it's violence against the *other* he's fantasizing about rather than against himself.

HL: Why didn't you actually say "*Fucking* shut up!"

JD: And run yourself through …

GN: … with a long knitting needle "a fool would shut up quick."

[*We decide it's time for another cigarette break on the porch. Upon return* …]

HL: So I made an observation during our smoke break. John and I discovered that we both, unbeknownst to each other, this summer were reading Anne Carson's [translation of] Euripides' plays and ironically enough we both read only the first two and the introductions. And we were talking about how she just took the plays and cast them in her own way – and I think that is kind of the same thing we're doing with this Oulipo Challenge. And I also made the observation that all three of us are treating the text neither irreverently nor reverently which I find …

JD: Yeah.

HL: And perhaps I'm the one most reverential because I'm the one using the most Shakespeare's original words compared to the others.

JD: But then there are turns where you …

HL: Yeah, there *are* turns.

PH: OK, shall we do the next chunk?

HL: Yes, we'll do number 5.

PH: Who would fardels bear,
   To grunt and sweat under a weary life,
   But that the dread of something after death,
   The undiscover'd country from whose bourn
   No traveller returns, puzzles the will
   And makes us rather bear those ills we have
   Than fly to others that we know not of?

GN: One more time?

HL: Do it better. Try and convey the meaning more. [*the Judge throws Hillar a dirty look.*] We saw that look. You just want to quickly go minus one.

PH: No, that's fine.

JD: If it's any consolation, I have been in that chair as Dramaturge before. It usually ends in tears by the end of the night.

[*The Judge rereads chunk 5.*]

HL: That's so much better. You're conveying the meaning. Thank you.

PH: We begin with Gregory.

HL: And it's also, by the way, it makes it more fun when you do a really good job cause it just kind of lifts the … It just puts it into context.

PH: I'm happy to oblige.

GN: Who would haul such a pack and groan and pant, Atlas
    as an ass,
    If not afraid of that commodity unknown,
    A distant land for which nobody owns a round-trip pass.
    In knowing this all priority shifts and spurs us onward
    with our load,
    Not by flight to unknown tribulation but by shuffling
    hoof on habit's road.

JD: Wow! There's a turn there. One more time.

HL: We're going to hear it again but can I just have the Atlas
line?

JD: Yeah, that's where the turn …

GN: "Who would haul such a pack and groan and pant, Atlas
as an ass"

HL: Atlas …

JD: … as an ass.

HL: … as an ass. *OH!* OK, I just conveyed my admiration.
Jesus!

GN: Thank you.

[*Gregory rereads chunk 5.*]

HL: shuffling "hoof"?

GN: The donkey metaphor.

HL: Gorgeous.

JD: Pulled all the way through, too.

PH: Hillar.

HL: For who would carry mighty loads
     to grunt and strain throughout our downtrod
     but that horror of mortuary's unknown –
     that mystical location from which
     no soul sails back – confounds our will
     and smacks us compliant to our daily ills,
     forbidding flights to simulacra still unknown?

PH: Again.

[*Hillar rereads chunk 5.*]

JD: That's lovely. That's my favourite of yours, actually.

HL: Is it?

GN: Yes, it's very lovely.

HL: Do you get this feeling they're getting better …

JD: Yeah.

HL: … chunk by chunk?

JD: Warming to the subject maybe.

PH: John.

JD: Who, through pools of doubt, paddling,
     Groaning to buoy this soul up,
     Though that iron pull down low waits to claim you?
     Imaginations unknown forms a-swim, on a mind's
     dimly lit floor,
     This no man can fly back to land from, manacling soul,
     will,
     And caging body within such bars of pain
     That thoughts of flight from a dying confound, and
     run to ground.

HL: Isn't buoy pronounced "booey"?

JD: Also, yeah.

HL: Both?

GN: Both.

HL: Can we hear it again? With "booey"?

JD: Sure.

HL: I think it sounds nicer. I might be wrong.

PH: Always the director.

HL: OK, just a moment, let me recover from that little snap there.

PH: You didn't have to take that negatively.

HL: No, but still, there's this little barking that seems to be going on from head of table and bottom of table.

GN: Oh, not at all.

PH: John.

[*John rereads chunk 5.*]

HL: "and run to ground"? As opposed to "aground"?

JD: Yeah.

HL: So you thought of "aground."

JD: Yeah. Almost like this juddering form of doubt.

HL: So, again, wow! Maybe this is the best of everyone's chunks because I loved what you did. And the "paddling," "pool." This is not a category but the … what's it called? Sound.

JD: Assonance?

HL: Assonance and the other word?

JD: Dissonance?

HL: No.

JD: Alliteration?

HL: Yes, the alliterative, the paddling in this pool and then you go from buoying to the iron and then you go back to manacle, right? So it's like …

PH: I agree that "booeying" is the better way.

GN: You just changed it syllabically though, buoy is one, "booey" is two.

JD: Exactly. Regardless.

HL: "Booey" is more airy as opposed to buoy which feels …

JD: Yeah. I'm trying to remember … Ken Garnham's play *Buoys*, …

GN: *Beuys, Buoys, Boys*.

JD: You've probably studied that by this point.

PH: I know it. I've read it but I haven't really studied it. I think I've done my mark.

GN: It's great you're doing this, man. Thanks a lot.

PH: No, it's a pleasure.

JD: You're hanging in there with great fortitude.

PH: Thank you. I'm doing my best. I'll be ready to eat shortly.

GN: Yeah, that lamb must be just bubbling away up there. It's going to be damn good.

JD: It's great to be back in this kitchen. After a year abroad isn't it a cool place to be again?

GN: Yeah. One of the first things I did when I got back into town was have dinner with Hillar. It was terrific.

JD: After close to ten years away from the city it's one of these places I just feel "I'm back!"

HL: Thank you. We've been through a lot in this room.

JD: Exactly.

HL: Tears notwithstanding. You know, this is ultimately *the* room, isn't it? This is where it all … Not that stuff doesn't happen elsewhere and, of course, in the summertime it's outside.

GN: It's the one I associate most strongly with ideas and long nights. There's something about kitchens. Do you have a nice kitchen where you live? Is it kind of a rallying point when people come over?

PH: A bit. It's a bit small. So it's hard to have more than one person in it.

GN: I love a big kitchen. You have dinner and then you end up with some candles and a bunch of people sitting around, just talking.

PH: OK, so chunk six. The final chunk. It sounds like a movie.

> Thus conscience does make cowards of us all;
> And thus the native hue of resolution
> Is sicklied o'er with the pale cast of thought,
> And enterprises of great pith and moment
> With this regard their currents turn awry,
> And lose the name of action.

Shall I read it again?

HL: Just for our pleasure. You're doing it better each time.

[*The Judge rereads chunk 6.*]

PH: So I believe it is you, Hillar, who begins.

HL: Thus such thinking cows us into cowards
and thus all plurality of plans
just drown in pallid casts of thought,
and notions of most profound gravity
all fail to grasp fruition
thus blasting us to crushing futility of inaction.

PH: When you're ready, again!

JD: Is it just me? But you have the most violent turns of fate.
Snapping back, just ripping the soul right out.

HL: I don't know. I hadn't thought of it that way. But yeah,
there are these ... swerves.

[*Hillar rereads chunk 6.*]

PH: OK, thank you. John, you're next.

JD: Thus a mind-manacling triumphs with us all;
And thus our sickly pallor of will
Colours all our thoughts,
And works to cut in stony epitaphs
Turn to dust
All flights of soul and mind run to ground.

HL: And your mark just got another "epitaph."

JD: Yes, fuck.

HL: Poor baby.

JD: Wow! It's …

[*John rereads chunk 6.*]

HL: Again this "running aground."

GN: Yeah. You use these recurring motifs. It's really interesting how you tie them together.

HL: A beauty, "Thus a mind-manacling triumphs with us all." Nice.

GN: That's a beautiful …

HL: In other words it's a noun, a "mind-manacling." Oh, that's beautiful. Are you sure that's grammatically correct – "and works to cut in stony epitaphs turn to dust."

JD: I should have put a comma there because "works" here is working as a noun rather than a verb.

PH: Gregory.

HL: Oh how exciting! The very last chunk! OK Gregory, smash us!

GN: Alas it is thinking and too much of it,
  That marks us out as cowards all.
  A hot fist thrust at oblivion's dark chasm
  Drawn back as cooling thoughts trump all.
  Bold plans of tumult and alacrity sway,
  And in this find many paths astray.
  Lost within this labyrinth of inaction's miasmic pall.

JD: Wow!

[*Gregory rereads chunk 6 and obliges us by repeating the last two lines.*]

JD: Beautiful.

HL: Gorgeous.

JD: Elegance. Elegantly done. Elegant variations.

HL: Just gorgeous.

GN: And you're going to read them all through too, right?

PH: Shall I do that? Or will you guys read your own all the way through?

HL: I think we should …

GN: Everyone read their own?

HL: Oh yeah.

JD: Yeah, I think that's …

PH: And when you say "Bold plans of tumult and alacrity sway," how are you using "alacrity" here?

GN: Immediacy.

HL: Speed, quickness.

JD: Expeditiousness.

GN: Expeditiousness. That's probably the best.

HL: That reminds me of when, decades ago, I was working as a telemarketer. There was a fellow there who told us this story – we're mailing out these books – and amazingly enough the person on the other end of the phone said – *And will you be mailing these out with alacrity?* And he said – *Alacrity is not in the office today.*

PH: I always thought of "alacrity" as doing something with ease.

GN: That was a delight hearing those … Now I can't wait to hear them all the way through.

JD: I know, I know.

HL: I have to say I'm really sorry about your E's.

PH: Was there an E in your last one?

JD: Yes there was.

GN: How many did you end up with?

JD: Three E's. It's time. I needed time to do another pass. That's what it is. That's my excuse and I'm sticking with it.

PH: Why don't we begin with John as he was the first one to begin?

HL: That was, by the way, one of the nice little symmetrical beauties of the six chunks. Everyone got to go twice first, twice middle and twice last.

GN: Always the director. Just one thing. As much as possible, because we read these in chunks, it would be helpful for me, if everybody's in agreement, that we try to minimize pauses between chunks, that we try to give the whole thing as much of a flow as we can.

JD: Great.

HL: Absolutely.

GN: Excellent.

HL: And I'll remind John to …

JD: … to read clearly. Yeah, pardon my voice. I'm just like gradually losing it.

HL: You were so loud when we were outside, I really noticed the fact that when we were having a cigarette your voice was booming away but then when you get inside, then …

JD: It's probably because in here I'm dealing with words I have to think about. OK, rather than jabbering on endlessly …

This daily dying or this nightly living; which prevails?
What if nobility lay in withstanding, all mind manacling
Wounds a man will sustain from want of luck's dark turns?
Or if it lay in arming his soul to fight such wild swings
of luck, night-born,
And brought to ground?
A daily dying; adrift on wormwood thoughts
All for nought; such drifting cast as final,
No hurt remaining, all such wounds
A body will withstand to mark a sum
This is a wish to tally.
A night-living; adrift on wormwood thoughts
Or such thoughts on wing, took flight from logic's grasp;
sadly
All ills of soul-sick living form from such flight
And at last burn out within a body, not a mark on it but
an Icarus scar,
Though such a firm FINIS should ground our thoughts
– for thusly
All days add up to nought but calamity.
For who could sustain a kind of faith within that long
spin of hours upon a clock,
Withstand wounds unjust, words struck from casts to
smash a proud man's will apart,
Or such a parody of amor fati that is romantic fantasy,
or a parodist's fantasy of a just world,
Or a revolt that's plainly just … though in withstanding all
A man may call this daily dying finally worth
His sacrificial nightly living,

With shiv in hand, why not?
Who, through pools of doubt, paddling,
Groaning to buoy this soul up,
Though that iron pull down low waits to claim you?
Imaginations unknown forms a-swim, on a mind's dimly
lit floor,
This no man can fly back to land from, manacling soul, will,
And caging body within such bars of pain
That thoughts of flight from a dying confound, and run
to ground.
Thus a mind-manacling triumphs with us all;
And thus our sickly pallor of will
Colours all our thoughts,
And works to cut in stony epitaphs
Turn to dust
All flights of soul and mind run to ground.

HL: What a mouthful!

GN: Do you need time to take notes in between?

PH: No. I think I'm OK. This has not been easy.

JD: This really is ridiculously hard.

PH: Yes.

HL: We've teased you about it but the thing also is … I think
it's fair to say none of us have sucked. If any of us would have
sucked your job would have been much easier.

PH: I also hope you are happy with my adjudications.

JD: Of course.

GN: I think you're doing a terrific job.

PH: Well, you haven't heard them yet, so … You might hate me at the end. In teaching, the first few weeks of class are wonderful, they love you and then you hand back the first assignment and the honeymoon is over.

GN: That's what it will be like when you actually give your scores to us.

PH: The honeymoon will be over.

HL: Yeah, we've been very friendly …

PH: You love me up until this point.

HL: I brought you an apple.

JD: A nest of vipers, that's what you'll be dining with.

All: Cheers!

PH: OK, so Gregory, you're next.

HL: Sorry, I need a touch more vodka. I feel like I can be a little more extravagant now that …

JD: … the pressure is off.

HL: He's going to give his results. Whatever. I think he's already warning us, he's basically starting to say – *Guys, don't expect any of you to get high scores.*

PH: Gregory.

GN: To act or not to act, this is our quandary
   Is our moral high-ground found by stoically rolling with myriad blows,
   That fortuitous position will attract,
   Or is it found through action, by mounting an attack,
   On a vast array of all that assails,

156

And by doing so, bring that array to naught.
Oh that I could avoid choosing and simply go rightly numb.
To blunt my waking condition at last
And spirit mind and body away from pain's many jolts and jabs,
Paroxysms born with my body.
A void, oblivion, a thing I fondly wish for.
But what of oblivion if in word only it stays,
A canvas not blank but full with somnambulistic illusions,
And additional acts of our plays.
What a bitch that is. For in a void what visions will visitations pay,
What traumas still to unfold,
As our corpora grind down to ash and clay.
Our minds hold onto this thought and in this way,
Our instinct to hang on through thick and thin holds us so taut,
That quixotic fancy cannot signal us astray.
For who would put up with such stabs and insults,
That mark our hourglass's sand caught fast in gravity's tug.
Bullying from landlord and boss, humiliations from big-shot dicks,
Conjugal bliss withdrawn and lost, fair conclusions not forthcoming,
Insults by official pricks.
Indulging fools unworthy as all of our clocks do tick,
Run through with a long knitting pin a fool would shut up quick.
Who would haul such a pack and groan and pant, Atlas as an ass,
If not afraid of that commodity unknown,
A distant land for which nobody owns a round-trip pass.

In knowing this all priority shifts and spurs us onward
with our load,
Not by flight to unknown tribulation but by shuffling
hoof on habit's road.
Alas it is thinking and too much of it,
That marks us out as cowards all.
A hot fist thrust at oblivion's dark chasm
Drawn back as cooling thoughts trump all.
Bold plans of tumult and alacrity sway,
And in this find many paths astray.
Lost within this labyrinth of inaction's miasmic pall.

JD: Mr. Beckett, can you give it to us in French now?

GN: With no E's.

JD: Wow! That's a lot of what I was hearing, it's almost like a channelling of Beckett.

GN: Thank you.

PH: Hillar.

HL: To stay on living or not: that is what confounds us.
Which would satisfy honour's most fair claim –
To sustain both slings and arrows of lunatic luck –
or to summon arms against a whirl of hardship
and by opposing, vanquish all?
To attain your infinity-long black-out –
that's all. And by that finality to stop
all soul-pangs, all manifold natural shocks
that physicality inflicts upon us, 'tis a consummation
to avidly long for.
To mortuary, to black-out -
to black-out: who knows, to host subconscious visions:
what a quandary!

For in that dormancy of black infinity what visions may
us haunt
as cast off is this mortal coil,
must halt our thoughts. This abiding doubt
marks with calamity so long a visitation in our world.
For who would stand unstopping whips and scorns,
subjugator's wrongs, proud man's opprobrium,
all pangs of ardour's snubs, law's crawl
and haughty authority's looks – only to wallow,
with calm mind, in unworthy's spurns,
not choosing to succumb to his finality
by committing swift hara-kiri?
For who would carry mighty loads
to grunt and strain throughout our downtrod
but that horror of mortuary's unknown –
that mystical location from which
no soul sails back – confounds our will
and smacks us compliant to our daily ills,
forbidding flights to simulacra still unknown?
Thus such thinking cows us into cowards
and thus all plurality of plans
just drown in pallid casts of thought,
and notions of most profound gravity
all fail to grasp fruition
thus blasting us to crushing futility of inaction.

JD: Beautiful.

GN: Bravo to both of you guys.

PH: Cheers to all of you.

HL: Congratulations to everyone. It hardly matters at this point
who …

PH: Beautiful, all. Really lovely. A pleasure to hear them.

HL: Thank you.

PH: Gregory, can I see your chunk two?

GN: Sure.

HL: This makes me feel like being in the Kiwanis [Music] Festival. This happened very rarely but you would have contestants one through fifteen play their fucking thing. And the adjudicator would do his thing.

JD: Did you have to go up and play a piece again?

HL: And every once in a while the adjudicator would sit back and say – *I would like to hear contestant number eight and number twelve once more.* And you thought it was all over, right? And now you have to go, BOOM, GO!

JD: *Brahms Piano Concerto number Four. All four movements!*

HL: There's a remarkable story about a fuck-up that happened and in order to fully understand …

GN: The Judge has this paperwork to do. Shall we go outside and have a cigarette and you can tell your fuck-up story outside?

HL: Sure. I will tell you my amusing story …

[The contestants all go out on the porch for another cigarette. Upon return …]

HL: OK, now it's time for the revelation. You're all familiar with the existence of Perec's *A Void*, the E-less novel.

JD: Yes.

HL: As it happens, and I don't believe this in any way is spoiling the novel, in the book is the *To be or not to be* soliloquy without an E. In fact this is what prompted the whole thing because I read it, then I got the original, meaning the Shakespeare and read it side by side and I said to myself – *You know what? I can do better than that.* And that is how the whole thing started.

JD: That's incredible. Wow.

HL: So basically I set it up as a challenge for myself and then I involved other people. Now, I have to say that obviously I never went back to the Perec and I didn't spend a lot of time with it upon first encountering it. And I will tell you right now the only thing that I remember of the Perec version is his take on the word "to sleep," which was "drowsy" and I thought – *Drowsy? That's not sleeping.* So I swear to you that I never went back to it and that was just the inspiration and that's the only thing I remember of it. It's not like me to ...

JD: Yeah.

GN: You wouldn't do that.

HL: No, I wouldn't do that.

JD: And, not to get pedantic about it, but it's also the translation of Perec from the French, which is the other thing, right?

HL: Yes.

JD: And you say to yourself that in the French it probably works a little bit better.

HL: Who knows?

JD: Yeah, who knows?

HL: So now I'm going to propose to you that I read it. I know that in my instruction I said that the Judge would read it.

GN: In French you could say *dormir* [to sleep]. You wouldn't have to worry about E.

JD: Exactly.

GN: You could say "sleep" easily. So probably the problems came in the translation rather than in the original.

JD: Yeah.

HL: So I propose now that I read it to you because I think I'm going to do a better job of reading it than our esteemed Judge.

GN: Do it better, Hillar.

HL: Well, this is not going to be very good because I haven't looked at it. This is the first time I'm looking at it since the summer.

> Living, or not living: that is what I ask:
> If 'tis a stamp of honour to submit
> To slings and arrows waft'd us by ill winds,
> Or brandish arms against a flood of afflictions,
> Which by our opposition is subdu'd? Dying, drowsing;
> Waking not? And by drowsing thus to thwart
> An aching soul and all th' natural shocks
> Humanity sustains. 'Tis a consummation
> So piously wish'd for. Dying, drowsing;
> Drowsing; and, what say, conjuring visions: ay, that's th' rub;
> For in that drowsy faint what visions may disturb
> Our shuffling off of mortal coil,

Do prompt us think again. Of that calamity, to wit,
That is our living for so long;
For who would brook duration's whips and scorns,
A tyrant's wrong, a haughty man's disdain,
Pangs of dispriz'd ardour and sloth of law,
Th' incivility of rank and all th' insults
That goodly worth from its contrary draws,
If such a man might his own last affirm
With a bald bodkin? Who would such ballast carry,
To grunt and wilt along his stooping path,
But that his horror of th' unknown,
That vast and unmapp'd land to which
No living man pays visit, is puzzling to his will,
Making him shrug off what now assails him
And shrink from posthumous ills?
Compunction thus turns all of us to cowards;
And thus our natural trait of fixity
Is sickli'd through with ashy rumination,
And missions of much pith and import
With this in mind soon turn awry,
And from all thoughts of action go astray.

Gregory, yours is better than that, John, yours is better than
that, mine is better than that.

GN: I think so.

PH: I would agree.

HL: And one of the things that I had not remembered … but
was very specific about at the time is you can't cheat with …

PH: … apostrophes.

HL: … with apostrophes replacing E's.

JD: We were outside and you [the Judge] weren't there at the time, you were still tabulating. But we were talking about Anne Carson's work and saying that she's both reverent and irreverent. I felt this was *really reverent* ... just going through and saying ...

GN: Well, what he's done is the bare minimum. He's kept every word that doesn't have an E in it and simply substituted words. He hasn't done a reconfiguring of it.

JD: Both reverent and formulaic.

HL: Yeah.

GN: It feels mechanical.

HL: Yes. And, by the way, guys, I appreciate you saying that because, as I said, my instinct was I can do better than this. And that's what inspired the whole thing. And then I brought you guys into it just because I thought the Perec was lame.

JD: Yeah.

HL: And did somebody say "perfunctory"?

JD: No, but that fits. It just feels ...

HL: ... stilted. It doesn't feel musical ...

PH: ... or poetic.

JD: Yeah.

HL: It feels strained and ...

PH: ... perfunctory.

JD: Yeah.

GN: That's the revelation?

HL: That's the revelation. I wanted to tell you this so now you know where it began from and that Hillar did not dream up this idea but that he read it and he just went – *You know what? No cigar.*

JD: Yeah, it's almost like you'd think he'd be far more bold considering what he was doing with this too. Like *A Void* is an undertaking, it's a whole novel so you'd think you'd be already in that state of mind where you're just fearless, you know.

HL: I'm just going to blurt this out. I think *A Void* has arguably some of the most spectacular writing I have ever encountered, period.

GN: It doesn't surprise me because I found just from my own experience, I would hazard a guess it was similar for you guys too, that with a restriction like that – and I guess this is the whole principle of the Oulipo – with a restriction so limiting it forces you to, what would you call it, lateral thinking? It forces you to explore areas that you might not … Because the first things you come up with may be forbidden by the rules so it forces you to think beyond and so it doesn't actually surprise me that a novel where that restriction applies all the way through would be so wonderful because the writer would be …

JD: That's what I mean …

GN: How can you constantly come up with different words and think differently about every line and …

JD: … and just fully engage with it.

HL: I'm very harsh in the sense that I'm very very careful with Gregory. When Gregory was gone all year, like literally from September 1 to August 21 …

JD: Right.

HL: I had to smile, by the way, when in your text was "round trip" … [*all laugh*] cause you *did* go around the world in one direction, right? I had a big smile inside me at that. Anyway, I do not recommend books to him lightly and during the time he was gone I spent a lot of time reading and I came up with three books that I said you *have to* read and *A Void* was one of them. And I also prefaced it with – *You have to let me start you off because I want to read you out loud the Prologue.*

JD: What other ones did you recommend?

HL: Naomi Klein's *The Shock Doctrine.*

JD: Yeah. I haven't read it yet but …

GN: *Parade's End*?

HL: *Parade's End.*

JD: Mr. Madox Ford.

HL: You haven't read it?

JD: I haven't read it yet, no.

GN: And I have to reread *One Hundred Years of Solitude* because Hillar read it while I was away and he wants to talk about it and I haven't read it for twenty years, so …

JD: Yes, it's been about that long for me too. I've come with a recommendation tonight too. I'm very close to the end of it but I'll save it for later. It's one of those where I'm just stunned by how good it is, but …

GN: What is it? You can't set it up and not say it.

JD: It's Vassily Grossman's *Life and Fate.*

HL: Uhuh. *New York Review of Books* published it?

JD: Yes.

HL: And have you finished it?

JD: Not yet.

HL: Oh, well then …

JD: So I can't …

HL: Exactly.

JD: I can't …

GN: But you're almost finished. I mean it's probably not going to …

HL: How many pages? 500? 400?

JD: It's about 870.

HL: And you're at page 700?

JD: Yes.

HL: Alright, well then the likelihood is …

GN: … it's probably going to be …

JD: … it's probably going to end well.

HL: But it *is* a challenge …

JD: It is.

HL: It is a challenge to go that last fucking …

JD: Yeah. And I've got caveats with it too but it's still … Oh my God.

HL: So, just to tease us, perhaps you could give us your marks chunk by chunk.

PH: OK.

HL: I think that would be funnest. As opposed to …

GN: I need another drink for *this*.

HL: I think that would be the most fun, don't you?

JD: Absolutely.

HL: Just to …

PH: … keep the suspense going.

JD: Keep the suspense going.

GN: You guys just keep talking. I'm just mixing a drink. Does anybody else …

HL: Yes.

PH: I think first I should just say that not only am I interpreting, in a way, your texts, but I'm also interpreting the criteria of the marks, right?

JD: Right.

PH: And in the last, "originality, ingenuity, brilliance, beauty and poeticism," there's a lot going on in that last one. So it was difficult in ways to assign that mark.

HL: Really?

PH: Yeah, because sometimes one would be so beautifully poetic which I would think earns a 3 …

HL Yes.

PH: … but maybe the ingenuity was …

HL: You know what? OK, maybe there's a little misunderstanding there. Because if you felt it was gloriously poetic, it's not like …

PH: Yes.

HL: What I meant was … that was a basket, brilliance, originality, ingenuity, poeticism, all of that is lumped together. So if you thought it was totally brilliant, you would give it a 3 even though it wasn't necessarily ingenious.

PH: And I did that at times but there are moments where … and this will come out and you can disagree perhaps.

JD: Right.

PH: So, the first chunk. The marks are: John, for accuracy I gave you a zero, for grammar a 1 and for the latter a 3 and you then lost a mark for an E so that was a total of 3 out of 5.

JD: OK.

HL: So for accuracy he got a zero?

PH: Yeah, I'll tell you why in a moment.

JD: OK.

PH: Hillar, 1 for accuracy, 1 for grammar, 2 for the latter, which brings you to a total of 4. Gregory, you got 1, 1 and 3 for a total of 5. For me … I thought, not for terribly long, but it was "this daily dying or this nightly living; which prevails?" I loved the poeticism of it but in comparison to Gregory's "to act or not to act." And Hillar, yours was …

HL: "To stay living or not."

PJ: There was something for me that was …

JD: … abstracted.

PH: It was abstracted to the point that … I loved the poeticism … When you were speaking about one's personality coming through, I thought to myself, yes, it would seem to me that you're a person who might take something and think – *I'm going to … not improve upon Shakespeare but to improve upon something, to take what possibilities you can to make it more beautiful in your …*

HL: You know what? I think you've hit on a very sensitive point.

PH: Yeah?

HL: I think that what we have done *is* better than Shakespeare. [*John laughs.*] I honestly believe that we have …

PH: Is that thing recording? [*All laugh.*] Hillar Liitoja just said …

HL: … that not only John's writing but everybody else around the table, we … caveats, of course.

JD: Yeah, give it a …

HL: In fact didn't I say so, something when you brought up criticism, I said – *I've got questions about your very first chunk …*

JD: Yeah.

HL: … *the beginning of it.* Because I just didn't buy it. And also the reason I've got a problem with it is it's the very beginning, it's the kernel.

JD: Oh, for sure.

HL: I mean "to be or not to be," "to stay on living or not," "to act or not to act" …

JD: I do think it is crucial too and I found it was crucial because it does lead me down ... I think if you nail it initially you're in the world of ... and [how I started it off] puts me into a level of abstraction there where I'm wrestling with this abstraction rather than Boom! It's *this* or it's *that*. And ...

GN: Also, it's one of those monumental lines in literature, that you can only play with to a certain point and then when you go off you're in ...

JD: And this is what I discovered, I think. I think part of it too was that contrarian streak where I said – *Fuck this. I'm just going to* ... And then I think probably around the second or third chunk I went – *OK, now I know why he nails it so. Because it grounds you.*

PH: And I even had a moment where I thought "being," "acting," what is the relationship there, right? But I deferred to that ... acting is a kind of living, living is a kind of acting, it's an action ...

HL: I mean, ultimately the question is ...

PH: ... it's a verb.

HL: ... do I want to continue living, in other words when we say "act," in this case it's "am I going to act to continue living or am I going to act in a way to kill myself?"

GN: That's just one interpretation. I believe that in this soliloquy, in fact, he is conflating action and being. Unlike Descartes' "I think, therefore I am," Hamlet is grappling with his inability to act, his procrastination which plagues him throughout the play. And I think that he's saying "to be" but it's *action* he's really talking about throughout the soliloquy. And the last word *in* the soliloquy is "action," he brings it all the way back.

HL: Can you please make your point again? I got it but I want to hear it again.

GN: I believe unlike Descartes' "I think, therefore I am," I think what Hamlet is saying here is you exist only through action ...

JD: Yeah.

GN: ... and that "I act, therefore I am."

HL: Thank you.

GN: So "to be or not be," to me, the whole thing is about ...

HL: ... am I going to act or am I *not* going to act.

GN: He's overthinking everything, he can't ...

HL: Yeah, and you had that also, the overthinking in your chunk 6.

GN: Just my interpretation. Just the way I see it.

JD: You're on pretty solid ground though.

HL: Action is being. OK, to make an extreme example I could be in a coma in a vegetative state and "I'm alive, therefore I am," I'm "being" – however that is rendered utterly useless by my inability to act and so therefore acting is an essential part of being.

JD: Yeah.

GN: According to Hamlet. And then he spends the rest of the soliloquy justifying inaction, saying – *Ah, but what about ... maybe I should just give up on all this and just die. But I can't die, I can't kill myself ...*

HL: … *because I'm scared of it.*

GN: … *because I'm scared of it. And I guess that's the reason we keep on living. But if we're going to live then we're going to have to act and I can't act.* Some people see it as a straight-up soliloquy about suicide. I don't. I think it's about …

JD: I don't think it is either.

GN: It's about his procrastination. It's about the fact he keeps getting the opportunity where he must act and he does not act.

PH: Cause even to take one's life is an action.

JD: This is it.

HL: Yes.

GN: Absolutely. And he's talking himself out of that as well, he's talking himself out of doing anything.

JD: I think it's with Shakespeare too and I don't want to go all of a sudden into Shakespeare criticism but everything is *clear* with Shakespeare when you go through it. Where all of a sudden he *is* abstracting things there's a fucking reason when he pulls that bodkin out and says – *This is it, it is that for sure.* Initially when I put "this daily dying or this nightly living" I had "this daily *living* or this nightly *dying*" to schematize it because what I wanted to go for was what he saw himself as … was his paralyzing thing, his self-consciousness. And then I said – *Well, it's the self-consciousness, the fact he has to be a performer every fucking day that is killing him.* So that's where the turn with "daily dying" came in. And then the conversations with his *real* self occur when he's … he can be authentic in himself in his subconscious, when he's *not* conscious, when he doesn't have to be an actor in this ridiculous situation that he's in. And that's how I was playing it. But it is absolutely true, as soon as you abstract to that level you can't bring it down again. It's almost like all of a sudden you've filled it up there and you just …

PH: The meaning changed for me, I guess, in a sense, the meaning changed at that point. Cause to say "this daily dying or this nightly living; which prevails?" … but is nightly living *dying*?

HL: Let me answer for John. I think what John is trying to say is: the way I'm having to live my life, day by day …

JD: … is a death.

HL: … whereas it's only at night, when I'm either alone or sleeping, that I'm liberated from all my duties and that's when I really feel alive.

JD: And of course there was filtering into that … most of his *real* conversations do occur with his father in that world so I do think that filters in. But it is the idea, really, that he is painfully self-conscious to a point where he can't act, as you say, he can't move forward with anybody.

HL: I want to go back to you, Gregory. I'm just trying to wrap my brain around your thinking. So you're saying "to be or not to be; that is the question" is not really about whether I stay alive or commit suicide, it's more like to act or not to act, in other words am I actually going to fucking do something, am I actually going to act in my mind's nobleness or am I just going to hang around and take all of this crap and …

JD: … and perform.

HL: … and perform and not be myself, not be my true self as Polonius told Laertes "to thine own self be true." Polonius got it right but said it to the wrong person.

GN: That's my interpretation.

HL: Thank you.

GN: I really do think that the entire soliloquy is a *rationalization of inaction*.

HL: Beautiful.

GN: He's justifying to himself … because death looms and we know not what might be there. His alternative to action is suicide but he can't do that. So he's constantly just buffeting back and forth. And at the end I think it's significant that the final word in the entire soliloquy is "action."

JD: Me too.

PH: And to kill myself is kind of the ultimate action.

GN: And he can't do that.

PH: Like "to live or not to live" – nothing else can happen if you're not living.

GN: Hamlet is painted in a corner here, he's got to *do* something. This is the desperate call that he's having now. It could almost be a mental breakdown – why can I not *do* anything? And then he rationalizes it all. I think that's …

HL: Beautiful.

JD: And in support of it, though, death isn't a *death*. There is a *reason* there's a fucking ghost in the play. It isn't a *death*.

GN: Exactly. The afterlife is present all the way through it.

JD: All the way through it. And this is what I meant by "the nightly living." It is not finality. There is a choice between actions, being true to the self or not. Death is not on the table for him as an option here, I think that's clear.

HL: Death is *not* on the table for him as an option.

JD: Death as finality here.

HL: Death as finality. OK. I think I've got it. Thank you for pointing out again the relation to the fact he's talking to his fucking father who's dead. So no wonder – I hadn't even thought about that – I mean it's very clear when I did HAMLET myself that I had all of the dead people … as soon as anyone died they were carried off but then they came right back and hung around. But yeah, no wonder he's going … Even though I did it in 1989 I feel like I'm understanding it differently, it's the same thing what we were talking about earlier, the difference between being 30 and 60.

JD: The only person who ends up speaking the truth to him is his father, who's dead.

HL: I think you're really right. I think you're probably right. Fortinbras enters after Hamlet's dead.

JD: That's right.

HL: What about Horatio? Horatio is more of a listener.

JD: Horatio listens to him.

HL: But he doesn't really give counsel.

JD: Yeah.

HL: From what I remember.

JD: And Ophelia speaks to him truthfully, but then …

HL: I was going to go to Ophelia next but Ophelia is … jangled, you know.

JD: Yeah.

HL: And she's problematic and she doesn't ...

JD: And you see where living in truth gets her. This is the thing.

HL: ... whereas his father is forthright.

JD: Forthright, direct.

HL: Waydago. I'm really proud of you. And this is just part of the glory of working on this because it's not a text that says "I went to the store, I purchased some apples."

GN: I entered it completely differently. I entered this exercise thinking it was a meditation on suicide and it was only working through it that I became convinced it's not. It's a meditation on procrastination. So the Oulipo exercise got me so deep into the text I began to think – *No way. This is* not *about suicide.*

HL: Wow!

GN: Suicide is a long list of things that require action that he cannot muster.

JD: Yeah.

GN: It's a justification for why.

HL: Incidentally, one of the things that has been successful about this is the fact none of us talked about it while working on it. Our take on it emerged with our versions ...

GN: Absolutely.

HL: ... as opposed to this round-table discussion about what does it mean.

GN: I think we all agreed we wouldn't have this conversation until it was all over, right?

JD: Yeah.

GN: That the big picture, theme ... we would just take the time to appreciate each other's take ...

JD: ... and then go ...

GN: ... then have the conversation. So that was 1 of 6.

HL: Shall we move on to #2?

PH: No, we haven't finished. I haven't told you why you got a 2 ...

HL: ... for poeticism and all that.

PH: Which I think is an important part of the discussion.

HL: Yes.

PH: So, your decision to use the same words, for me, that goes against the ingenuity a little ... one has to be very ingenious to make new words, to *not* depend upon the original words so I felt that in the same way that there was a penalization for a lack of accuracy that I had to go to the other end and say that a lack of ingenuity needs to be ...

JD: That's the polarity.

PH: So I wonder if ... because there's so many – originality, beauty, poetry, ingenuity – there was so much going on that it was difficult not to ... I think that some of these points should be broken out if you were to do it again.

JD: Yeah.

HL: Ahaa. Separate it. In other words, decide which of the five ... and then go a point for poeticism, a point for brilliance, ingenuity, whatever – as opposed to lumping them all together.

PH: There's just too many things to take into consideration there.

JD: For sure.

HL: OK, good.

PH: But "vanquish all," I thought was so poetic and beautiful it was difficult for me not to give you a 3 on that.

HL: I don't blame you.

GN: It was very beautiful.

HL: I really like my "lunatic luck."

PH: Yes. Chunk 2.

HL: Roast too.

GN: I think we have a few more minutes before we need to check that again.

PH: Chunk 2. John received 1 for accuracy, 1 for grammar, 3 for originality *et al* and minus 1 for an E for a total of 4.

GN: Top score, though.

HL: I'm so sorry for your E thing. I just feel that … it's fair but I'm just sorry.

JD: We're old enough to …

PH: Hillar received 1 for accuracy, 1 for grammar, 3 for everything else, for a total of 5. Gregory received 1 for accuracy, zero for grammar, 3 for everything else for a total of 4. It seemed to me that unlike all the other chunks – tell me if I'm wrong – but the grammar sort of went out the window on this one.

GN: May have. I respect your analysis.

PH: Whereas most of the time I think you're paying attention to the grammar, there was almost no grammar in this one, there's one semicolon I think …

GN: Oh yeah, I was bad with putting the punctuation …

PH: No, it wasn't just that.

GN: That's totally fine. I think that chunk does need a little bit more work to make it grammatically smooth, so …

PH: "To die, to sleep; to sleep, perchance to dream." And you go "Oh that I could avoid choosing and simply go rightly numb. And to blunt my waking condition at last."

HL: That sounds correct to me.

PH: Right, but the grammar of "To die: to sleep"; … he's working it out whereas this seemed to me more just almost a question, "Oh that I could *do* this" …

JD: Right.

PH: … but not a working out in the same way.

JD: Right.

HL: I think the point about grammar is – is it correct grammatically?

PH: Are we talking about sticking to Shakespeare's grammar or correct grammar in general?

HL: Correct grammar in each person's version.

PH: OK, cause I wasn't thinking in that way.

HL: I think the point is each person's version has to be grammatically correct as opposed to …

PH: But the poetry often goes against rules of grammar. Do you mean make sense, grammatically make sense?

HL: I think grammatically correct, that sentences have the verb, the subject goes with the verb …

PH: OK, yes, then perhaps that should change the mark because I was thinking with regards to addressing the grammar in Shakespeare's text.

HL: Oh well, dock him for ingenuity then. [*All laugh.*]

GN: That's OK, I'm fine with that.

PH: Well, I think that if this is the …

GN: I think we discussed it earlier, the criteria of grammar. And that was the idea that what the person has written is grammatically correct.

HL: Yes.

GN: Not so much that you followed the grammar of the original.

HL: Exactly.

PH: Well, then all of you were grammatically correct across the board.

GN: Were there any glaring moments where the grammar didn't work?

PH: No.

GN: Well, then …

PH: OK, then that means Gregory gets a 5.

HL: Good.

JD: *Bon.*

HL: Hey, I just fought for you.

PH: Again, I thought it was the fidelity of the grammar of the …

HL: You want to make sure to change it on your collation.

PH: I will. I'm going to have to go through the collation again.

GN: Beautiful.

HL: Number 3.

GN: By the way, thank you so much. This is just great. You've really listened and taken great notes and had great ideas about the stuff. That's so helpful.

PH: No problem.

HL: Great instinct to invite him to be Judge. And lovely that you have risen to the occasion.

JD: It's a punishing role too.

PH: But obviously not thankless. So chunk #3. John, accuracy 1, grammar 1, originality 3, so full marks; Hillar, 1, 1, 2 again for the ingenuity. And also I felt like this one wasn't as poetic as the other ones. It wasn't as beautiful as everything else you had done. Maybe I'm wrong.

HL: You know, I thought "mortuary" was good and I also thought "blackout" was good and I also ...

GN: Hillar, now we brought in this Judge to make judgments.

HL: I'm allowed to defend myself.

PH: Absolutely.

HL: I just defended *you*, hello?

GN: We were talking about grammar there, rules. This is interpretation.

PH: I didn't like "blackout" to be totally honest.

HL: OK. But "in that dormancy of black infinity" ...

JD: I liked that too.

HL: I really liked that.

PH: That was nice.

HL: OK, good enough.

PH: And then I had the grammatically correct moment which I was interpreting wrongly, cause I have Gregory 1, zero, 3.

GN: But I'm getting zero because I didn't stick with the grammar of the original text?

PH: Yes. Not because it wasn't grammatically correct.

GN: And in that regard I would probably get zero all the way through because I pretty much abandoned the ...

PH: There was a difference in different moments. Sometimes you stayed more connected and other times you didn't and that was what I was struggling with. OK, shall we move on?

GN: Yes.

PH: For chunk 4 everyone got 5 except you, John, had an E so you have 4. I thought your "upon the clock" was lovely. Gregory, your colloquialisms and rhymes were wonderful.

GN: Thank you.

PH: And Hillar, yours was beautiful and poetic although I'm not sure, is hara-kiri swift? That was just a small question.

HL: Oh yeah.

PH: You have to put it in, pull it across?

HL: I believe there's a three-move thing that happens and generally you *do* have someone who is close with you to actually chop off your head.

JD: You ever see *Mishima* [the film]?

PH: Yeah.

JD: That's how he does it.

PH: I just think of it as a most horrible and painful …

HL: It *is* horrible and painful but it's swift.

GN: It's all about thrusts.

PH: That wasn't a criticism, it was just a question.

HL: Are we in number 5 now?

PH: We're in chunk 5 now. So the marks were: Gregory 1, 1, 3; Hillar 1, 1, 2; John 1, 1, 3. Again with the ingenuity, why "grunt" and then "strain" rather than "grunt" and … what was Shakespeare's other word?

HL: "sweat"

PH: Because of the E, right?

HL: Yes.

PH: But "grunt" – I wanted a new word.

HL: Aah! [*All laugh.*]

PH: I wanted ingenuity cause that was part of the challenge, right, it wasn't just to ...

JD: To be fair, it *is* one of the things with Perec we looked at and said OK ...

GN: That he kept all the words that didn't have E in them.

JD: But I didn't think you did a lot of that. I'm just saying ...

HL: Yeah, it wasn't like I'm constantly doing that.

PH: No.

HL: I am using ... but I don't feel like ...

PH: Hillar is going to hate me now.

HL: No, I'm not going to hate you. But I just don't think that ...

PH: I thought ingenuity was so difficult to do. And leaving in a Shakespeare word that doesn't have an E seemed in some way a little bit of a way out. I don't mean to ...

HL: You're making me think of cooking shows where, if I was a judge, I've actually seen this, you don't have to fuck with *every single element*, you know ...

PH: Right.

HL: ... just like you don't have to *prove* like you can do ...

JD: I needed that coach to tell me that, actually.

PH: But I loved the "smacks." And "mystical location" – beautiful.

HL: Great. [*heavy sarcasm*]

PH: John, your "through pools of doubt, paddling" and the swimming, the way that works all the way through – beautiful. And Gregory, the "ass" and the "hoof" and "the road" …

JD: I loved the alliteration of the "ass" and …

PH: … and "the commodity" and then no one owns it …

JD: Yeah.

PH: … which was really lovely.

GN: Thank you.

HL: I had difficulty with "commodity," the "undiscover'd country" being a commodity.

GN: The *unknown* "commodity."

JD: There was only one word in your whole piece that I fought with and that was "priority." For whatever reason it stuck with me. I think it was in the course of a line cause each line was so …

GN: "In knowing all this priority shifts"

JD: The only word that stuck with in the sense where … just another term or something …

PH: Chunk 6. Perfect scores all around except for …

JD: The E again?

PH: The E. OK, so now I must go through my math again.

HL: Well, it's very simple. Gregory wins, I come in second and John comes in third. Not sure what the point is to get the *exact* score. We should look at the roast.

GN: Yeah, that's what we should do.

HL: Congratulations, Gregory! Waydago!

All: Cheers! [*much glass-clinking*]

GN: Thank you so much. Thank you. It was so much fun.

JD: I'll do that again.

GN: Well, we all win.

PH: I don't feel like I'm winning right now.

[*All laugh. Hillar and Gregory check on the roast; the lamb sirloin is ready; soon the table is set, wines opened and the feast begins.*]

Postscript

I find it a particularly piquant irony to discover, years after the event, that the whole Oulipo Challenge was inspired by a text non-existent in Perec's original!

You might remember John wondering if Adair's translation-mediocrity had something to do with it *being* a translation – but then suggesting that did not make sense seeing as Perec's entire endeavour was so bold, his approach so fearless, it seemed inconsistent for him to produce such a flaccid version of the great soliloquy. Something was not quite right.

Well, John was right. After finding out Ian Monk had translated but never published his version I mailed him several questions. His speedy reply set me straight –

The first thing that needs clarifying is the status of the 'to be or not to be' passage in the novel. If you remember, the idea is that the characters come across an anthology of poetry, which they read, sense to be rather bizarre but fail to spot what is amiss about it. In the original French, Perec rewrote e-lessly a selection of very well known (to French people) poems by Victor Hugo, Baudelaire, Mallarmé and Rimbaud. Adair, rightly or wrongly (it's a very debatable point) decided to replace these pieces by rewrites of well known English pieces, the choice of which pieces of course being his own. Personally, I think he was wrong to do so, because the characters are French

and not British, but as I said his decision can be defended, on the grounds that it gives readers of English a similar experience to that which French speakers have when reading these rather strange versions of familiar poems. The next debatable point is then, of course, Adair's choice of pieces to treat. The 'to be or not to be' soliloquy is certainly one of the best known pieces in the corpus, but what is it doing in an anthology of poetry? Then comes the problem that he quite clearly failed to find a way to do it which stayed close enough to the original for readers to have to blink a little before seeing what was going on (which is the whole point of the endeavour). For these reasons, I think Adair was wrong to do what he did.

And for all these reasons, I didn't choose to do what he did, but instead translate Perec's rewrites of well-known French pieces in my unpublished translation. I produced this when still unknown and just weeks before the publishers signed with Adair, which explains why my version was not published. I now find it to be too juvenile to show anyone. Sorry.

What a surprise it was to read this revelation – concerning my own "revelation" within the Challenge! And also a thrill to find Perec's honour unsullied!

* * *

Even more shocking was to hear back from Olivier Salon after I'd sent him our three transliterations. I had warned he would find them tough going seeing his English was not that strong. I had also asked him not to think us total idiots: we were aware John's version had an unfortunate three E's but at least mine and Gregory's were E-free. He replied he had read them but his – *English is not good enough to judge and compare them. I have not enough vocabulary!* This was not surprising, however it is difficult to express my stupefaction's extent upon reading the continuation –

I can only say that the first version (John Delacourt) has 6 E's! the second one (Gregory Nixon) one E (in the last verse) and yours one E (those pangs).

I wish you a very nice day,
Olivier

I was trembling, shaking, quaking with horror! I had made a fool of myself in front of an Oulipo member. Have "a very nice day"? I felt crushed, my self-esteem shattered. I grabbed Gregory's chunk 6 and read it through *thrice* in a row, each time more carefully. I could not find an E. By this time I was so distraught I could not even locate the word "those" in my own text.

An hour later I mailed Olivier – with the rather accurate subject-line "losing my sanity" – and begged him to cut and paste both my and Gregory's E-lines as well as the undetected John's lines. Though never having met he acted like the truest friend. Realizing the depth of my bewilderment – re-reading the email I sent him confirms the frantic despair I conveyed – he responded *immediately* with irrefutable proof: our three complete versions with all E-words coloured orange along with a pleading assuagement –

Stay safe and sane, please! It's not a drama! it's not a fault! I know all of you has worked a lot.

Sincerely yours,
Olivier

Calm slowly began to descend. I stared at those ugly *petites carottes* and made myself a drink. But I was still flummoxed. How was it possible three intelligent highly-literate people could not espy E's flaunting themselves in plain view when the cardinal principle was to banish them? How could our Judge, a professor of theatre, allow E's to become like neutrinos continually passing through our bodies without trace or effect? And what had happened to otherwise-reliable Magda once given an E-meter?

* * *

This issue, hard to believe, became even more vexing. When I finally got around to making a word-for-word transcript, another little gem lay awaiting. In order to eliminate reader-confusion I decided to omit three lines from the "official" transcript – yet here is what transpired directly after John read his fourth chunk, with restored lines in bold:

HL: OK. You've got an E in there, baby.

JD: Whereabouts?

HL: Towards the end. Or middle.

JD: "revolt."

HL: Yeah.

JD: And "one" as well.

PH: Oh-oh.

HL: There you go.

JD: Oh, God! What the hell is going on? I'm going completely off the fucking reservation with this.

HL: Nicely put. Accurate assessment.

JD: Yes.

So another E had been teased out from hiding. But not for long. It was wont to disappear once again. Some twenty minutes after the above back-and-forth, directly after we finished chunk 5, there was a little break as Gregory and I got some wine and put bottles in the back unheated room to chill. During this interval our Judge began tallying up his marks for chunk 4 – and then the following rather astonishing exchange (fully omitted from the "official" transcript) ensued with John –

PH: You said that in the last round you had two E's.

JD: Yes.

PH: You did? I didn't find them though. "revolt" and …

JD: … somewhere else.

PH: Or did I? [*Paul re-checks his notes.*] No, I didn't find the second E.

JD: Let me see. [*John goes through his chunk 4 text.*] "revolt," yeah, and … umm … hmm …

PH: I think there was only just the one E.

JD: I think you may be right. Let me just see here. [*John goes back to his text, even reading part of it out half-loud.*] Yeah, I don't see it either.

PH: OK, you know what, I've done my marks for this chunk.

The above exchange lasted for about a minute. Though focused entirely on finding that elusive second E throughout those last 45 seconds, neither John nor Paul succeeded in so doing – yet that same E had not only been already *found* some minutes ago, it was also in the same *line* as the fixated-upon "revolt," a mere three words later!

* * *

After considerable contemplation, always knowing I did not wish to deceive the reader, I decided to take all undetected E-words out of the actual versions and replace them with uninfected substitutes – and then own up to the truth in a postscript. I thought the most interesting outcome of this Challenge was our wildly differing soliloquy-mutations with the E-issue of secondary importance. As suggested a moment ago, I decided in favour of suppressing reader-confusion – *Why is the Judge saying there was only one E in this chunk when, in fact, there are two?* – while admitting I may have deprived the most attentive readers a particular glee – *Wait a minute. This word has an E and they just completely missed it!*

Here now are the lines you read in the "official" transcript followed by those actually presented at the Challenge, with the undetected E-word underlined:

Gregory, chunk 6, last line –

Lost within this labyrinth of inaction's miasmic pall.
Lost within <u>the</u> labyrinth of inaction's miasmic pall.

Hillar, chunk 4, line 3 -

all pangs of ardour's snubs
<u>those</u> pangs of ardour's snubs

John, chunk 4, line 4 -

> **Or a revolt of all that's plainly just**
> **Or a revolt of all <u>one</u> knows as just**

John, chunk 5, line 5 -

> **This no man can fly back to land from**
> **This no man can <u>return</u> to land from**

* * *

I now bid farewell to that issue which has, ever since receiving Olivier's oranges, frustrated, perplexed and tormented me – I speak, of course, of my inability to understand our shared obliviousness regarding those pesky irritating E's. I thought of writing all three Oulipians I am in touch with, asking if they might shed experience-garnered luminosity. Is our incompetence simply a product of inexperience, that hoary "practice makes perfect"? Should we have gone Harry Mathews' route and fastened thumbtacks, with pin up, to our keyboards' E's? I was afraid I had no choice but to admit the insuperable nature of this comprehension-quest and conclude with a plea to the gods – *Please let these E's stop haunting me and let my mind turn to other things.*

Yet strangely enough, only a couple of hours ago, while worrying this postscript, I feel as though I have finally landed on an explanation both satisfying and sensible. Perhaps less strangely, the solution had been flirting in front of me in the form of an answer to a question posed to Magda, who often has the distance or clarity unattainable by myself.

Before I proceed with what I promise to be my final "revelation" permit me a few observations. Of course our inexperience with lipograms was not helpful though one might think the countless hours spread over months would have done the trick – at least for Gregory and myself as it later turned out John began work on his version only some hours before leaving home for the Challenge. Alcohol was not to blame. Though we were drinking throughout out colloquy it was in moderation with no diminution of mental acuity, no slurred speech. Utterly beyond me, however, is why I never thought to press Control F and type in E – a solution inelegant but infallible. I note how non-flushed-out E's occurred in words most innocuous (one, the); how John's blind spot most often occurred when the rejected letter followed "r" (prevails, remaining) and how all those words transmit strong power (revolt, return); how none of us truly disgraced ourselves with adjoining E's or multiple-E words.

When I asked Magda why she caught an early E of mine but missed the later one she didn't have to think for long – *I know you told me to focus exclusively on the E's but I couldn't help it. I got caught up in the text.* And that seems to be the most plausible explanation for all of us. Of course we were all avoiding E's and then trying to ferret them out. But after awhile the mind, unbeknownst, imposes its own will and switches over. E-avoidance was the challenge we all failed at – however the *real* challenge was to think through Shakespeare, to interpret and then recast his words, to convey his thoughts' essence in ways both new, poetic, musical, perchance even ingenious. Ideas-expression trumped E-hunting. Pride of lovely phrase-turn created E-invisibility. Yet no matter how felicitous some of our dodges and twists, no matter how vertiginous our over-precipice-leanings before last-moment pullbacks, what remains is proof of our status as noble amateurs over whom tower the Olympian Oulipians.

About the Author

W ishing to emulate Glenn Gould, and after graduating from U of T with a Bachelor's in Piano Performance, Liitoja realized the futility of his quest. After some misery and despair he embraced a new idol in Ezra Pound and founded DNA Theatre, initially to propound his work in a unique fashion, then moving on to create a wide range of performances dealing with AIDS, Artaud, installations and ballets. Recently he was awarded an inaugural Kathy Acker award in recognition of both his continual determination and commitment, over 35 years, to create ground-breaking, unconventional, provocative experiences, all the while taking daring risks.